W9-BLL-023

3 1611 00289 8416

100+
WAYS TO
Recognize
&
Reward

YOUR SCHOOL STAFF

100+ WAYS TO Recognize & Reward YOUR SCHOOL STAFF

Emily E. Houck

GOVERNORS STATE UNIVERSITY
UNIVERSITY PARK, IL

ASCD

Alexandria, Virginia USA

1703 N. Beauregard St. • Alexandria, VA 22311-1714 USA
Phone: 800-933-2723 or 703-578-9600 • Fax: 703-575-5400
Website: www.ascd.org • E-mail: member@ascd.org
Author guidelines: www.ascd.org/write

LB
2842.22
.H68
2012

Gene R. Carter, *Executive Director;* Ron Miletta, *Interim Chief Program Development Officer;* Richard Papale, *Publisher;* Laura Lawson, *Acquisitions Editor;* Julie Houtz, *Director, Book Editing & Production;* Deborah Siegel, *Editor;* Judi Connelly, *Senior Graphic Designer;* Mike Kalyan, *Production Manager;* Cynthia Stock, *Typesetter;* Andrea Wilson, *Production Specialist*

Copyright © 2012 ASCD. All rights reserved. It is illegal to reproduce copies of this work in print or electronic format (including reproductions displayed on a secure intranet or stored in a retrieval system or other electronic storage device from which copies can be made or displayed) without the prior written permission of the publisher. By purchasing only authorized electronic or print editions and not participating in or encouraging piracy of copyrighted materials, you support the rights of authors and publishers. Readers who wish to duplicate material copyrighted by ASCD may do so for a small fee by contacting the Copyright Clearance Center (CCC), 222 Rosewood Dr., Danvers, MA 01923, USA (phone: 978-750-8400; fax: 978-646-8600; Web: www.copyright.com). For requests to reprint or to inquire about site licensing options, contact ASCD Permissions at www.ascd.org/permissions, or permission@ascd.org, or 703-575-5749. For a list of vendors authorized to license ASCD e-books to institutions, see www.ascd.org/epubs. Send translation inquiries to translations@ascd.org.

Illustrations © Johanna Kindvall

Printed in the United States of America. Cover art © 2012 by ASCD. ASCD publications present a variety of viewpoints. The views expressed or implied in this book should not be interpreted as official positions of the Association.

All web links in this book are correct as of the publication date below but may have become inactive or otherwise modified since that time. If you notice a deactivated or changed link, please e-mail books@ascd.org with the words "Link Update" in the subject line. In your message, please specify the web link, the book title, and the page number on which the link appears.

PAPERBACK ISBN: 978-1-4166-1474-6   ASCD product #112051   n11/12
Also available as an e-book (see Books in Print for the ISBNs).

Quantity discounts: 10–49 copies, 10%; 50+ copies, 15%; for 1,000 or more copies, call 800-933-2723, ext. 5634, or 703-575-5634. For desk copies: www.ascd.org/deskcopy

Library of Congress Cataloging-in-Publication Data

Houck, Emily E.
  100+ ways to recognize and reward your school staff / Emily E. Houck.
    p. cm.
  Includes bibliographical references and index.
  ISBN 978-1-4166-1474-6 (pbk. : alk. paper)
  1. School personnel management. 2. Incentive awards. 3. Employee motivation.
4. Motivation in education. I. Title. II. Title: 100 plus ways to recognize and reward your school staff.
  LB2842.22.H68 2012
  371.2'01—dc23
                                                                          2012025983

23 22 21 20 19   18 17 16 15 14 13 12 1 2 3 4 5 6 7 8 9 10 11 12

*This work is dedicated
to my first teachers—
my parents.*

Contents

Preface

I received a copy of this letter (see Figure A) that was sent to my superintendent by my principal 23 years ago. Obviously I still have that letter. Why would I have saved this acknowledgment of my efforts so very long? It's simple; it was something special, unexpected, and extremely rare, and in retrospect, sad. Sad that it was so out of the ordinary, that it became a one of a kind keepsake. How different I would have felt if I had worked in an environment where the acknowledgment of my efforts was commonplace, where I knew every day that I was valued and what I did was making a difference. Who knows, I might still be there.

The goal of this book is to help you move your department, school, or district into that kind of place—a place where acknowledgment is appreciated, but is not a once in a lifetime event.

Praise isn't a foreign concept. It isn't difficult to dispense, but a jaw-dropping 65 percent of Americans report that they have never received any recognition for their good work on the job. Consequently they leave. We can change that in the business of education. We can increase individual productivity and increase engagement among colleagues. We can retain our teachers,

FIGURE A
A Recognition Letter

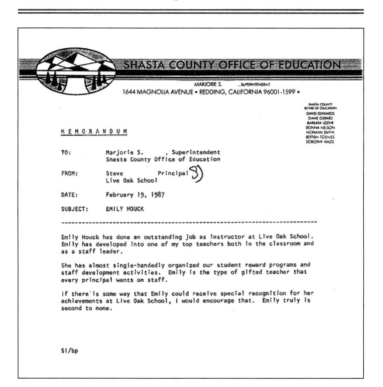

encourage staff loyalty, and increase parent satisfaction by recognizing the hard work and effort of colleagues and our educational staff members.

This book is intended to provide administrators, department heads, classified managers, and anyone heading up a group of people with practical, easy to use, and inexpensive or free ways to motivate, reward, and recognize the efforts of their staff.

As a side note, I never heard from the superintendent.

The Top 20

These 20 ideas (see Figure B) are my favorites from the book. I have used them all with great results.

Figure B
Top 20 Recognition Ideas

Idea	Effort	Page
A Visit from the Past	Moderate	69
Aahhh!	Moderate	71
Ask Their Opinion	Moderate	72
Friday Focus	Moderate	78
Good Job Parents, Good Job Teachers	Low	32
Immediate Feedback	Moderate	87
Involve Them, Empower Them	Low	36
Make That Call	Low	40
One-on-One	More	118
Pay Them/Shake Them	More	119
Put Pen to Paper	More	122
Sweet Treats	Low	51
Table Topper	Moderate	99
Tell the Boss	Moderate	101
Tell the Story in Pictures	Moderate	101
Tell Us What You Think	Low	54
Thank the Parents	Low	57
There's More to Schools Than Just Teachers	Low	61
Tongue Depressors	More	128
You Are	Moderate	104

~ 1 ~

What Employees Want

**There are two things people want more than sex and money. . .
recognition and praise. —Mary Kay Ash**

This section of the book will be kept relatively short, so you can get to the "good stuff" quickly. But I think it's important to touch on why recognition and praise are important in the workplace, even if it's just a brief overview.

Research tells us that employees want some specific things from their jobs (Blanchard & Bowles, 1998). These are

- The ability to provide for their families and themselves
- Control of achieving a goal
- Worthwhile work
- Recognition of staff efforts and accomplishments

Most of us don't have much control over paychecks, so we'll pass over that the first one and move on to control of achieving a goal.

Control of Achieving a Goal

"When teachers were asked, 'What is it that makes you so outstanding?' they readily remarked that they had an administrator who encouraged and supported them, trusted their professionalism, and made them feel like a significant member of a very important team."

—Neila A. Connors

In his work, Maslow talked a lot about reaching levels of belonging and esteem (Podmoroff, 2005). Teachers and staff members having a say in the development of the school or district goals falls nicely into supporting the development of these needs: belonging and esteem. When teachers are in a positive environment, one in which they are contributing towards the common goal, they are more apt to share their fulfillment with their students in a win/win situation. "Purpose is a powerful motivator. The inherent recognition in purpose comes from seeing progress towards goals" (Ventrice, 2003, p. 25). Sharing a common goal and working towards its attainment doesn't just benefit the individual person; it is a major contributor to school growth. Additionally, it is one of the leading factors as to why teachers stay at given schools or in the profession entirely.

Simply stated, folks that work in schools don't want to be treated as unthinking drones. They want to be part of the plan, they want their input to be heard, and they want their ideas to be taken seriously.

Worthwhile Work

"People have to understand how what they do contributes to the well-being of mankind."   —Blanchard and Bowles

We spend nearly one-third of our adult lives at work, so it stands to reason that we want our workplaces to be a source of need fulfillment. When that happens, our lives are full and enriched, and we can focus our attention on finding meaning through work. When it doesn't happen, we are so preoccupied with finding other ways to satisfy our needs that we are never truly present at work (Podmoroff, 2005).

As educators, we can easily understand the importance of our work. In our young people, we nurture academic talent, mold behavior, increase occupational choices, develop civic accountability, and encourage personal maturity. In sum, we shape the future.

We cannot assume, however, that all our school staff members feel appreciated in this work, and we should not take their efforts for granted. Instead, we should highlight and recognize their contributions to the present and the future, both because it is the right thing to do and because it will motive them to continued excellence. Whitaker argued in *Motivating and Inspiring Teachers: The Educational Leader's Guide for Building Staff Morale,* "Principals who take the time necessary to make sure that teachers understand their worth will find that classroom instruction will improve as teachers' self-efficiency improves" (Whitaker, Whitaker, & Lumpa, 2000, p. 188). We have all experienced the joy and honor we feel when a former student finds us and lets us know that we've made a difference in their lives. That's why we teach, that feeling. Administrators and other leaders can harness that commitment and passion by reminding our staffs that they matter.

The contributions teachers make to the development of young people is readily apparent. We must also remember to recognize and reward the other members of our staffs whose contributions remain hidden from obvious view. Our cooks, custodians, bus drivers, and secretaries also matter in the quality of a school, and we must strive to also highlight and publicize their efforts and achievements.

Recognition of Staff Efforts and Accomplishments

"Administrators who make it a priority to treat teachers with respect, recognize invaluable contributions, and realize teachers are their best allies, see great things happen." —Neila A. Connors

If we want to keep our quality employees and those energetic young teachers, we need to make sure that we are meeting their needs. Recognizing and rewarding their efforts helps. Many teachers start their careers working hard and excelling, but if over time their efforts go unappreciated and unrecognized, even the most dedicated and creative teacher will fade into the background (Podmoroff, 2005).

With one-half of teachers leaving the profession within the first five years, we need to reflect on what causes this loss and what can be done to reduce the loss of the young, ambitious employees that come into the profession. More than half of those leaving cited unsupportive principals as a factor in their decision to leave—we can change these conditions. We can make our employees feel supported and involved in shaping their work lives.

If your efforts to increase morale, motivation, and recognition are embraced by your staff, then they will know that you care about them as professionals and as individuals. This sense of caring will lead to greater achievement by both your staff and your students (as a product of the staff's efforts). "With the right recognition, you will find employees more willing to tackle problems on their own instead of bringing them to you to solve. With the right recognition, employees will show more concern about quality and reputation. With the right recognition, employees will be more willing to pitch in when things get difficult" (Ventrice, 2003, p. 3).

- 2 -

Elements
of Recognition

**The best executive is one who has sense enough to
pick good people to do what he wants done, and
self-restraint enough to keep from meddling with
them while they do it. —Theodore Roosevelt**

B efore we delve into the main elements of recognition, we
should debunk a few myths. When we ask administrators
to recognize members of their staffs they generally raise
four excuses. Dianna Podmoroff outlined the following myths:

1. *I'm an upbeat person, so I can motivate my people.* This
implies that someone else can motivate you. You can't motivate
others, but what you can do is create a motivating environment
for each of your staff members. A motivating and supportive
environment can cause employees to motivate themselves
towards a more productive performance.

2. *Fear is the best motivator.* Some managers believe that
the fear of losing their job is motivation enough to keep a staff

producing. In the education arena, this belief misses on three points. First, fear will only work for a very short period of time. Second, fear creates a hostile workplace, which leads to a higher than usual turnover of staff, which is never good for children. Third, after teachers earn tenure they no longer fear losing their job for underperformance. As a result, a fear-filled workplace creates only resentment and unhappiness, rather than performance and achievement.

3. *I know what motivates me, so I know what will motivate my staff.* This is wrong on a couple of levels. What motivates one person does not necessarily motivate another, and what motivates today may or may not motivate the same person tomorrow. An educational leader needs to know which factors will promote and nurture professional growth in each individual.

4. *Recognition of some will cause jealousy and tension among the staff.* This can be a real problem if the recognition is viewed as favoritism. Leaders can avoid this pitfall by having clear criteria for the recognition and then recognizing employees for meeting those criteria. Consistency is critical. Don't confuse this recognition with the simple thank you. Thank yous can and should be given out freely. Just as human sensitivities about salaries do not prevent people from picking up their paychecks, sensitivities about recognition should not stop the structuring of recognition programs and events (Podmoroff, 2005).

In general, we can divide recognition into four elements: praise, thanks, opportunity, and respect.

Praise

What is praise? Simply put, to praise is to recognize and to commend a job well done. It reminds recipients that the quality of their efforts matters, and it shows them that their good work is noticed and appreciated. If praise is to be effective, it needs to be tied to five elements. Praise needs to be authentic, specific, immediate, clean, and private.

What does *authentic* praise mean? It's simple—it means that you praise your employees for actual accomplishments, and that you don't make up things just to offer them some positive strokes. You don't have to worry about giving out too much praise if you make sure that the recognition you give is earned. Your employees will know when you are making stuff up merely to recognize everyone, and no one will feel that they are praised too much or too often if it is for something genuine.

Your praise needs to always be *specific*. Just as we teach our instructors, you have to tell the person why they are being recognized in a very specific way. Describe the behavior you are recognizing when giving recognition. For example, instead of saying, "Thank you. You did a good job," say, "Thank you for leading our textbook committee. Your talents brought a tough group to consensus." Specificity indicates that you really do know precisely how the employee contributed and highlights the particular behaviors that are praiseworthy.

The need for *immediacy* is rather self-evident. Provide your recognition shortly after the deed is done. It certainly loses much of its potency when you wait weeks or longer to recognize someone's efforts. Immediate might not be possible, but sooner is better than later. Immediate praise is important for at least two reasons. First, it signals true respect for the action and the actor because it requires us to rearrange our priorities to make the praise happen now rather than waiting until it's convenient for us. If it's praiseworthy, it's worth praising now. Second, in order for praise to shape behavior we need to intervene immediately with gestures that support and affirm. Don't let days or weeks go by—weeks that might be filled with grumblings of resentment—before offering praise.

Keep it *clean*. The term "clean" isn't quite as clear. It simply means that you shouldn't tie anything to the recognition. It should stand on its own. In particular, never tarnish praise with criticism. For example, clean praise states: "Great job heading the report card committee. You guys did great work and your leadership kept them on track." Do not blemish this praise with criticism such as, "But next time maybe you could speed up the process a bit." It would have made it unclean and diminished its effect.

The last element of praise is *private*. Experts disagree on this point. Some follow the maxim "Praise in public, criticize in private," while others maintain that your praise should also be done in private until you have the person's permission to publicize it. However, you can have it both ways by offering anonymous praise in public. This allows you to recognize the accomplishment without unwanted pointing of fingers. An example might be saying at a staff meeting, "Thank you to all of you who got your report cards turned in on time. It meant a lot to the office staff."

If you are not convinced that praise is the way to go, consider this quote from Todd Whitaker's work: "Which is more likely to keep you on a diet—someone saying, 'Boy you are really looking good!' or the comment 'It's about time…'"? (Whitaker, Whitaker, & Lumpa, 2000, p. 31).

Thanks

A sincere thank-you is a highly effective form of recognition. The simplest and most desired form of recognition is a simple expression of gratitude. Simply stated, thank your staff for their efforts.

Does that mean you should say thank you for everything everyone does every day? No, not necessarily. If what they do makes your job easier or if it makes a difference in the lives of your staff or students, say thank you. It will go a long way toward promoting a positive environment.

There are many ways to give thanks, and they can be very simple or elaborate in nature. Simple can be appreciated as much as any elaborate message. Putting a thank-you into a written form can be seen as a grand gesture. Have you gotten a note from an employer and kept it? A simple note in written form expressing gratitude or pride is, in my opinion, the most powerful form of recognition. Mix it up—start simple with an oral thank-you, and move toward more complex or elaborate avenues such as a written note, paying thanks in situations where it wouldn't be commonplace, making a home phone call to express your thanks, and holding special events to show your appreciation.

Opportunity

Giving opportunities is a subtle yet very valid form of recognition. Ask staff members for their opinion on how things should be done, let them voice their opinion on critical issues, and include them in decision making. All of these give them the opportunity to participate at a meaningful level. What a level of recognition you'd accomplish if you allowed your employees to select their own professional development courses and seminars. Give them the opportunity to determine what skills they need to develop.

When a teacher comes to you with a request to try a new approach in his or her class, you can recognize them as professional by giving them the opportunity to try new things. Finding funding to do projects, taking trips, or exploring a change in techniques sends a message that you believe in them and their ideas. This is inherent recognition that is built into the workplace.

Respect

"Employees want to be valued, not just for what they can do, but for who they are" (Ventrice, 2003, p. 19). We need to consider our employee needs as we make decisions and recognize them as valued assets to our schools, districts, and profession.

There are several ways to demonstrate to your employees that you respect them and what they do. Does your staff have the resources to do their jobs? Teachers having to reach into their own pockets to buy supplies for their classrooms is a subtle way to tell them that what they do isn't important to the district. They might think, "If the district thought more of me, then they'd support my program." Funding is always scarce, but it is important to know that an administrator who is unwilling to look for resources sends the message that the employee's ideas are not respected.

Beware if the school is dirty, is in disrepair, or is unsafe! Unsafe, unappealing workplaces suggest to the employees in those workplaces that they don't matter much and that they don't deserve better. In other words, show respect for your employees by providing for them an appealing workplace. Almost one-third of the teachers leaving the profession cited unsafe and unclean environments as a reason for their departure. How people feel in their environment is as important as any other factor when looking at job contentment. Staff may not see these things as recognition. However, they will see a troubled environment as a lack of recognition of their value to the organization, and many will leave because of it (Ventrice, 2003).

The simplest way to respect members of your staff is to ask their opinion about the operations of your school or district. "What can we do to improve our reading program?" "Do you have any ideas how we could streamline our bus runs?" "Do you think all-day kindergarten is good for kids?" Administrators who make it a priority to treat their staff with respect, recognize invaluable contributions, and realize that teachers are their best allies will see great things happen (Connors, 2000).

You can demonstrate respect with simple, yet powerful actions. Try these:

- Treat people with courtesy, politeness, and kindness.
- Encourage coworkers to express their opinions and ideas.
- Listen to what others have to say before expressing your viewpoint. Never speak over, butt in, or cut off another person.
- Use people's ideas to change or improve work. Let employees know you used their idea, or, better yet, encourage the person with the idea to implement the idea.
- Praise much more frequently than you criticize. Encourage praise and recognition from employee to employee as well as from the supervisor.
- The golden rule does apply at work, or, as professional speaker Leslie Charles says, "Implement the platinum rule: treat others as they wish to be treated."

~ 3 ~

Wrapping It Up

I cannot teach anyone anything.
I can only make them think. —Socrates

D on't put recognition on your to-do list. It shouldn't be treated as any other task—not one you can cross off and be done with it. Recognition is a mind-set—a way of doing business and of relating to people every day. With a different way of looking at things, you can find ways to recognize folks in every employee interaction.

As you begin to prioritize recognition, bear in mind some basic tenets. Be consistent. You don't have to give everyone the same recognition or reward, but you do need to be fair. Recognition doesn't need to be the same, indeed it shouldn't be the same for all recipients, but it should have value consistent with the value of the contribution. Keep it up. Commit to recognition for the long haul. Frequent gestures of appreciation and esteem are more important and more sustainable than rare grand gestures.

What happens if we view recognition as a luxury? What if we don't commit to improving the morale and performance of our staffs? What difference will it really make if we don't take the time to validate their efforts? There is a consensus among researchers and educators that the single most important factor in determining student performance in school and in life is the quality of his or her teachers and the instruction they provide (Wong, 1999). Therefore, if it is our goal to provide the very best for our children, it is essential that we concentrate on retaining high-quality teachers in every school across the nation. Recognizing their efforts will help make them want to stay.

For those of you who like numbers, let me put it another way. A conservative national estimate of the cost of replacing public school teachers who have dropped out of the profession is $2.2 billion a year. If the cost of replacing public school teachers who transfer is added, the total reaches $4.9 billion every year. For individual states, cost estimates range from $8.5 million in North Dakota to a staggering half a billion dollars for large states such as Texas (Alliance for Excellent Education, 2005). Recognition of your staff efforts can turn this around. It energizes a school. It creates loyal, motivated, and positive-thinking staff members who pass their enthusiasm on to their students. In addition, managing and leading a motivated staff is certainly easier than the alternative.

When we value our employees as people, it is easier to get them into the right mind-set. Find positive things in what people do, rather than spending your time looking for what's wrong. You'll find with this mind-set you'll have just as much to do, but it will be much more fun and rewarding for you and your staff.

Why is this important to you as a leader? Think of the times you have tried to get a staff to adopt a new program or to embrace a new way of doing things. A staff that knows you have their best interests in mind and trusts you is bound to be more willing to try new programs and ideas, even if they are skeptical. In turn, staff members who try new things, who push themselves, are more likely to reach educational excellence than those who remain stubbornly committed to the status quo. Recognizing and cheering on your staff is in their best interest, in the best interest of their students, and in your best interest as well.

~ 4 ~
Low-Effort Ideas

Low-Effort Ideas

Item	Page	Thanks	Praise	Respect	Opportunity
A Bit of the Grape	20	x	x		
Attendance Raiser Award	20	x	x		
Babysitting Services	21	x			
Balloon Surprise	22		x	x	
Bravo Cards	23		x	x	
Break Bread: Strengthen Bonds	23			x	x
Brush Off	24	x			
Business Cards	24			x	
Can't Talk About Work	25			x	
Caught in the Act	25		x		
Certificates	26	x	x	x	
Clean Out Those Files	29			x	x
Employee of The Month	30		x	x	
Family Smiles	30	x	x		
Go Fly a Kite	31			x	
Go Put Your Feet Up	31	x	x	x	
Gone Fishing	32	x			
Good Job Parents, Good Job Teachers	32	x	x	x	
Great News	34		x		
Happy Birthday	34			x	
Hide and Seek	36	x	x	x	
Involve Them, Empower Them	36			x	x
Jeans for a Day	37	x	x	x	
Key Contributors	38	x	x		

Item	Page	Thanks	Praise	Respect	Opportunity
Let It Grow	38				X
Let's Eat	39	X			
Light Up Their Lives	39		X	X	
Make That Call	40	X	X	X	
Me Bag	40			X	
Meeting Agendas	41	X	X	X	
No Food, No Meeting	41	X		X	
No Interruptions	43			X	
Perk Up	43	X			
Pizza Anyone	44	X			
Plan a Staff Field Trip	44			X	X
Planning Days	45			X	X
Pot Luck	46	X			
Report Card Reward	46		X		
Reserved Parking	48	X	X		
Say Cheese	48	X	X		
Send Them Away	48			X	X
Spread Rumors	49		X		
Spread the News	49		X		
Stand Up	50	X	X		
Superintendent Visit	50	X	X	X	
Sweet Treats	51	X	X		
Tell Us What You Think	54	X	X		
Thank the Family	57	X	X		
Thank the Parents	57	X	X		
Thanks a Lottery	60	X			
There's More to Schools Than Just Teachers	61			X	X
Unexpected, The	61		X		

Item	Page	Thanks	Praise	Respect	Opportunity
Wall of Fame	62			x	
Wal-Mart Cheer	62		x		
Welcome Them	63			x	x
Working in Your Pajamas	63			x	x
You're Appreciated Notes	64	x	x		

A BIT OF THE GRAPE

Praise, Thanks

A nice bottle of wine can be an appreciated recognition of a job well done. (It doesn't have to be expensive, but definitely do not give wine in a box.) After being given the wine, the employee should to take it immediately to his or her car. Alcohol on campus or at the district office is not a good idea. You need to know your staff because this reward may not be appreciated by or appropriate for everyone.

Needed: *a bottle of wine*

NOTE: Just because this item is first doesn't mean I advocate using alcohol as a reward above other types of recognition. It's first simply because it comes first alphabetically. Cheers!

Date Used: _____Recipient: _____

ATTENDANCE RAISER AWARD

Praise, Thanks

Every month, ask your school secretary to calculate the attendance rate for each classroom. The class with the highest attendance rate each month can win a pizza party, and the teacher should be rewarded as well. If the teachers buy into the competition, either for the "glory" or for the reward, they will then make phone calls or encourage students to pick up their attendance. This then improves the school's overall attendance rate and increases funding. Everyone wins.

You may wish to put a minimum attendance rate on the contest. For example, the class must have an attendance rate of at least 90 percent to qualify. This competition can be used to encourage improved attendance between schools or grade levels as well.

Needed: *Some type of reward that can be used for an entire class. Examples—pizza, doughnuts, ice cream, extra free time at lunch, no homework for three days.*

NOTE: If you go with a food reward, consider making a partnership with a business. If a pizza place provides pizza once a month, your students will provide art for their walls or windows, for example.

Date Used: _____Recipient: _____

BABYSITTING SERVICES

Thanks

This idea is ideal for rewarding your staff members who have young children. You can say to a teacher: "You did a great job on such and such; let me reward you by giving you a night off."

Develop babysitting coupons that the staff members can turn in for an evening of free baby sitting. You can do the babysitting yourself or you can work with your student council to provide the service. The staff member will have to give adequate notice for this to work, but an evening out without the kids can be a great reward.

"Oh, we couldn't do that."

"You've been working so hard on our WASC accreditation; you and Tom deserve a night out without kids. Let me say thank you by doing this for you."

"You're the best! Are you sure? We'll just go out to the movies or something."

"Take all the time you want. The kids and I will be fine. I'll bring over my son and they can play together. Go."

With this reward the hardest part is getting them out the door, particularly if the kids are babies. Bringing one of your own kids can make it more of play date, instead of you doing babysitting duty.

"Thank you for the wonderful night out. It seemed like I hadn't seen my wife in ages. This was a most thoughtful gift." Dave, 10th grade English teacher

Needed: *A list of students who would provide babysitting services. Make sure you have an extensive list, so you will always have a student available, even when there are sporting events and other school functions.*

NOTE: The Red Cross in some areas offers babysitter certification classes. If your students were certified it might make the parents more comfortable.

Date Used: _____Recipient: _____

BALLOON SURPRISE

Praise, Respect

Cover the teacher's desk with balloons. Either tape the balloons to the surface of the desk, or fill the ballons with helium and tape their strings down. Attach notes to some of the balloons recognizing the employee's efforts.

Having a tank of helium in the office is a great asset. You'll find you have lots of opportunities to use it. A year's tank rental is very nominal. The company might even donate a tank to the school if you ask.

Needed: *balloons, string, helium tank, tape*

Date Used: _____Recipient: _____

BRAVO CARDS

Praise, Respect

Sometimes simple is best. This idea works for anyone in a leadership role, from superintendents to department heads, and from PTO presidents to the human resource director.

Have cards made up with the word "Bravo" on the front and nothing written on the inside. When you see something that deserves recognition, write a brief description on the inside with a note of thanks and send it to person you want to recognize (Nelson, 1994).

Needed: *cardstock, color printer*

Date Used: _____Recipient: _____

BREAK BREAD: STRENGTHEN BONDS

Opportunity, Respect

I like this one!

Take your new teachers and their spouses to dinner before school starts. By dining as a group, the teachers will then have others at school they will know when school starts. This connection will make the first few days less scary. Breaking bread together is one of the best ways to develop bonds between people.

If you are doing this as a superintendent, invite all of the new teachers from the district AND their site principals.

Needed: *restaurant reservations*

Date Used: _____Recipient: _____

BRUSH OFF

Thanks

Here's a quick and easy way to say thank you to your staff, whether it's an entire district or just a few bus drivers.

If you prepare the notes in advance, you can spring into action anytime a "Brush Off" is needed. On those days that it snows during school hours, get 10 or 12 students to invade the teacher parking lot right before dismissal time and brush off their windshields, leaving a note, "You have been brushed off by a member of Student Council."

"It was late and cold and I was tired when I headed out the door to go home. Imagine my surprise and delight to find my windows scraped free of snow and ice. What a treat. You can't imagine how much I appreciated your kindness. Thank you." Note sent to the student council from a grateful teacher.

I had someone suggest to me an alternative to this idea for those who don't live in the snow. That idea is to bring in a tire company and have them rotate the tires of the staff. They might do it for free if you let them put a flyer on the windows.

Needed: *hand brush, cardstock, laminator*

NOTE: You'll need to laminate the notes you put on the windshields or they'll be destroyed in the snow. Additionally, make sure you have extra helpers so you have enough helpers when school activities come up.

Date Used: _____Recipient: _____

BUSINESS CARDS

Respect

Order business cards, or make them up yourself, for every staff member. What your teachers and staff members do for society and the district is ultimately important and they deserve to be treated as any other important business person. They deserve to have their own business cards to hand out as they see fit.

Needed: *business cards*

Date Used: _____Recipient: _____

CAN'T TALK ABOUT WORK

Respect

Hold a faculty gathering or department meeting where teachers cannot discuss education, students, or the administration. Anyone overheard discussing these topics must put $1.00 in a basket, with proceeds going to the sunshine fund (Connors, 2000). This works very well if you go to a local restaurant or tavern after work, or even to a home of a staff member.

Needed: *Fund basket*

Date Used: _____Recipient: _____

CAUGHT IN THE ACT

Praise

Put this on the agenda of every staff meeting as the last item.

Ask staff members to share positives things about other staff members. These can include things done at school to help a student or another staff member, or things done outside of school. For example: "Congratulations on winning the community tennis tourney," or "Thank you for helping me develop a lesson," or "I know Sally put in lots of extra time and effort to help Juan pass his economics final." You may have to start the ball rolling by offering up a "Caught in the Act" first. This is a way to offer a simple thank you or recognition to their colleagues (K. Wheeler, personal communication).

Date Used: _____Recipient: _____

CERTIFICATES

Praise, Respect, Thanks

Present an award or certificate to the recognized employee at a board or staff meeting. Don't be limited to these few examples. Make up your own. You'll find a few sample certificates in Figure 4.1.

• **Antelope Award: We're better because you are here.** This award can be given when you want to recognize the outstanding work done on a daily basis by one of your employees. Of course you would need to customize it to match your school's mascot.

• **Highly Qualified Teacher Certificates.** Many times teachers have had to jump through a lot of hoops to get themselves "Highly Qualified" in the mind of the government. By providing this certificate you recognize their efforts and their professionalism.

FIGURE 4.1
Certificates

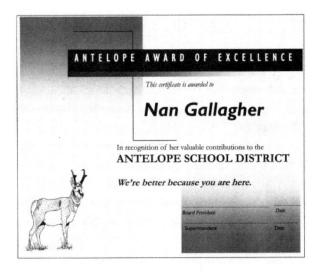

FIGURE 4.1 (*continued*)
Certificates

Highly Qualified

Faith Rogers

has met all of the requirements set forth
by the State of California
and is hereby certified a
Highly Qualified Teacher
in the area of mathematics.

Signed this 27th day of February 2006.

_____

Dr. Emily E. Houck, Superintendent

PERFECT ATTENDANCE AWARD

This certificate is presented to

HELEN HERD

*for achieving perfect attendance for the
2009-2010 school year.
Your dedication is appreciated and it has
made a difference in our school.*

Superintendent	Date	Principal	Date

They'll post these in their classrooms and it will serve as an assurance to the students and parents that the teacher is a professional.

• **You Make a Difference Award.** This award is printed with a starfish in connection with the fable repeated below. The company Master Teacher sells Starfish pins that can be given with this award. Present this award to staff members who make a difference in your school or district.

Starfish

As the old man walked the beach at dawn, he noticed a young man ahead of him picking up starfish and flinging them into the sea. Finally catching up with the youth, he asked him why he was doing this. The answer was that the stranded starfish would die if left until the morning sun. "But the beach goes on for miles and miles and there are millions of starfish," countered the other. "How can your effort make any difference?" The young man looked at the starfish in his hand and then threw it to safety in the waves. "It makes a difference to this one," he said.

—Author Unknown

• **Badge of Courage Award.** Encourage and reward "coloring outside the lines" by your staff. It takes courage to try something new, even if it is for the good of students. Recognize that effort and the leap by giving this award to your risk takers.

• **Perfect Attendance Award.** We recognize students for perfect attendance, why not our staff members? It takes an effort on their part to be there every day. Let them know you noticed. A gift certificate for a family dinner is a good reward. It's more than just the teacher getting to work—it's a team effort or a family thing.

• **Apple Award.** This can be used as a catch-all award. You can tailor it to fit any need you have for recognition.

Don't stop at just giving the award; even if you have given it out in a public arena, you can take it a step further and let the community know about all of the good works of your staff. Several times a year, take out a full-page ad in your local newspaper and recognize all the award winners for a given period of time.

Needed:

- *You need either fancy certificate paper or a printer so you can print your own.*
- *I suggest some sort of pin to commemorate the honor. Check out the company Master Teacher for ideas.*
- *A camera to capture the moment.*

NOTE: Send these awards in to the local newspaper. Many times they'll publish a picture and a short article about the honoree, particularly if you write it for them.

Date Used: _____Recipient: _____

CLEAN OUT THOSE FILES

Opportunity, Respect

Consider giving this reward to a teacher who has had a hard couple of days or weeks. It'll give them a chance to catch their breath.

Give a "Clean Out Your Files Day" to a deserving teacher. The teacher is still working so he or she isn't counted as absent but is free to do something he or she always intended to do but never did. This activity can revitalize a person. The teacher will undoubtedly find some "treasures" to put into use in the classroom.

NOTE: You will need to get a substitute for the teacher's classes that day.

Date Used: _____Recipient: _____

EMPLOYEE OF THE MONTH

Praise, Respect

A word of caution with this form of recognition—because it doesn't recognize a specific task or accomplishment it can be seen as a bit gratuitous. It may have the intended effect on the employee and it may not. If it is an award that everyone is going to get eventually, the employees who are honored late in the year and praised for their great work may not feel honored. It may be perceived the same as being picked last for a team in gym class (Rath & Clifton, 2004).

If you choose to recognize your staff in this manner, I suggest that you only use it when you have a large staff so it isn't given out to everyone.

Needed:

- *Certificate paper to write on or a printer to print out your own certificates*
- *Commemorative pin for the employee*
- *A camera to capture the moment*

NOTE: Send these awards in to the local newspaper. Many times they'll publish a picture and a short article about the honoree, particularly if you write it for them.

Date Used: _____ Recipient: _____

FAMILY SMILES

Praise, Thanks

School principals, here is one just for you.

Arrange to have the photographer of your school pictures take a family portrait of a deserving staff member. You could do this for everyone at a minimal price as well. This is a gift that will last much longer than a candy bar.

Needed: *a photographer*

NOTE: Have your secretary call the family and remind them of their appointment.

Date Used: _____Recipient: _____

GO FLY A KITE

Respect

Teaching can be very stressful at times, and one of the greatest ways to recognize teachers is to recognize their stress level and provide ways to ease the strain. Try handing out inexpensive kites to the teachers at a staff meeting and go outside and enjoy the adventure of kite flying instead of dealing with the planned agenda.

Needed: *kite kits, string, rags (for the kite tail), wind*

NOTE: If you decide to make the kites instead of buying pre-made ones you'll probably have even more fun as the activity of making the kites can be a hoot. This way the teachers can also personalize their kites.

Date Used: _____Recipient: _____

GO PUT YOUR FEET UP

Praise, Respect, Thanks

Cover the class or classes of a teacher and give him or her the afternoon off. Make sure the teacher goes and does something fun or relaxing and doesn't go do school work!

Date Used: _____Recipient: _____

GONE FISHING

Thanks

Fish-shaped crackers can be combined with any of these sentiments for a nice and simple acknowledgment.

- We're hooked on your great attitude.
- Your dedication is "fin-tastic."
- Your team commitment makes a big splash.
- Your attention to detail is clear to "sea."
- You dive into every task with enthusiasm.
- Your efforts make a whale of a difference!

Needed: *crackers, card stock*

NOTE: Make up a few extras to keep on hand for parent volunteers or other outside helpers.

Date Used: _____Recipient: _____

GOOD JOB PARENTS, GOOD JOB TEACHERS

Praise, Respect, Thanks

This is an idea for superintendents to help them connect more to their staff, but all leaders could incorporate it.

Many of your staff members are parents and are proud of their own children's accomplishments. Acknowledging their part in their own children's success is a nice way to recognize staff. The accomplishment doesn't have to be a grand success—it could just be a significant milestone. Examples include graduating from college or graduate school, completing basic training, or landing a good job. I recommend doing this in two parts. First, send the parents a letter of recognition when you get word of the accomplishment. Second, write about the accomplishment in the staff newsletter. This last part recognizes the accomplishments of the school staff and lets them know that what they do, and did, does indeed make a difference. See Figure 4.2.

Needed: *paper and a little time*

Date Used: _____ Recipient: _____

FIGURE 4.2
Letter of Recognition

SCOTT SCHOOL DISTRICT
P.O. Box 687, 11918 Main Street, Anytown, CA
Phone: 530-468-xxxx   Fax: 530-468-xxxx

6/30/2012

Mrs. Alex Hayes
15308 N. Hwy 3
Anytown, CA

Dear Alex:

Congratulations!

I heard through the grapevine that your son, Ryan, is a very recent graduate of law school. I know parents influence their children and I wanted to acknowledge your part in supporting him and his decision to help others through the law. The curiosity and giving nature that you instilled in him is a gift he will be using for the betterment of the world. Thank you for the effort you have put forth and for sharing him with us as a student in our schools. We too are proud of his accomplishments, and I believe we provided him with a solid foundation upon which he built his future. The Scott Valley schools are good ones, and Ryan is an example of that.

Again, congratulations. Well done, Mom!

Sincerely,

GREAT NEWS

Praise

In Figure 4.3, you will find an example of a way to spread recognition into your community. When you see an article in the local paper about someone in the community who has a connection to your school—a parent or business member—simply cut out the article and attach it to this graphic. Write a brief note and mail it to the person. I have gotten a few of these and really appreciate the thought and effort that went into sending me the note.

Needed: *access to local newspapers*

Date Used: _____Recipient: _____

HAPPY BIRTHDAY

Respect

Go into a teacher's room or the staff's work area on the chosen staff member's birthday and have the kids join you in singing "Happy Birthday" to the honoree. It's fun for the kids and will make the staff member smile. Confetti is always a nice touch.

Send birthday cards to your employees' homes. You can also send an e-card—it's not as personal, but it is expedient and is an easy way to make sure you actually meet the deadlines.

I remember receiving a birthday card from my superintendent while I was still teaching, and it made a definite impression on me. While I realized that he did that for everyone, I was still impressed that a guy with his job would take the time to think of me. I never forgot that kindness, and I have continued the celebration by sending a card to each of my employees on their birthdays. While Mr. M. (my superintendent) sent a real card through the post office, I have to admit that I send them

FIGURE 4.3
Recognition

GREAT NEWS

IT'S ALWAYS A PLEASURE TO READ GOOD NEWS
ABOUT PEOPLE IN OUR COMMUNITY!

All of your friends at the Scott Valley Unified School District office were
pleased to see this item and we send our best wishes to you!

Attach newspaper clip here

Include handwritten note here

electronically using an online service. The thought is still there and is still appreciated.

Needed: *the birth date of all employees, confetti, birthday cards*

Date Used: _____Recipient: _____

HIDE AND SEEK

Praise, Respect, Thanks

This one is quick and easy, and fun for the recipient. It can be initiated by any school leader.

Write on five or more sticky notes thanking the person for a job well done and hide them on or in their desk or lesson plan book. It'll be the gift that keeps on giving throughout the day. (Nelson, 1994)

Needed: *sticky notes*

Date Used: _____Recipient: _____

INVOLVE THEM, EMPOWER THEM

Opportunity, Respect

An excellent way to validate your teachers' expertise is to encourage them to share their knowledge and skills. As a part of each staff meeting, have a teacher give a "curriculum share." This involves teachers giving a brief presentation (5 to 30 minutes) to their peers on an instructional technique that works for them or on a curriculum topic. Our teachers have a lot to share if we just would ask them. Rotate the responsibility throughout the staff. Every teacher should do at least one curriculum share every year.

If you believe in your teachers and they know you do, they'll shine and improve your school.

Too many times we only see individuals as experts if they have to travel 50 miles or more to present. It has always been a mystery to me why traveling seems to make what someone has to say more important. We have experts on our own staffs. We need to acknowledge their value and utilize their expertise. Members of your staff can be used to design professional development opportunities, to suggest speakers, and to be expert presenters.

NOTE: Make sure that the teachers have advance notice of their presentation dates. I recommend that you have the teachers sign up at their first staff meeting. Post the list in the staff room, and send out e-mail reminders. Just in case someone forgets, it's always prudent to have a lesson up your sleeve that you can deliver to fill in if necessary.

Date Used: _____ Recipient: _____

JEANS FOR A DAY

Praise, Respect, Thanks

Declare a "Wear Your Jeans to Work Day." It's nice to show your human side every once in a while, and most people like to wear their jeans and be comfortable. It also sends the message that it's not okay to wear them on a regular basis.

To make this day a reward for staff members who have gone above and beyond, have stickers printed that say "I earned this Jeans Day" and allow the person to wear their jeans on the day of their choice. (http://michiganprincipals.org/masc/staff_appreciation.htm)

Needed: *pre-made "I earned this Jeans Day" stickers*

Date Used: _____ Recipient: _____

KEY CONTRIBUTORS

Praise, Thanks

Recognize staff members for making a "Key Contribution." Buy large gold skeleton keys. Create a certificate and present it and the key to parents, staff, or community members who do something significant for your school or district. (K.C., La Conner Middle School, Washington, http://www.wacaonline.org/resources_staff.html)

Needed: *large cardboard keys, certificates*

NOTE: You probably can get pre- printed large keys at party decoration stores.

Date Used: _____Recipient: _____

LET IT GROW

Opportunity

For school employees who live in cities or don't have access to garden space, the school can set aside space on campus for spring and summer staff gardens. Employees can grow their own plants, flowers, or vegetables. If you're lucky, they'll share part of the bounty with you or even with the school kitchen.

Needed: *pre-laid out and sized garden spaces*

NOTE: Make sure the staff members know that they need to provide their own seeds, plants, and tools.

Date Used: _____Recipient: _____

LET'S EAT

Thanks

Here's another one where we get to eat.

Order a party pizza or huge sub sandwich for a communal lunch. Breaking bread is at the top of the list of ways to bond a staff. Put a note in the bulletin or post a sign to give advance notice to your staff that you are providing lunch on your chosen day. You don't want them to opt out because they brought their own lunch from home.

Needed: *party food*

Date Used: _____Recipient: _____

LIGHT UP THEIR LIVES

Praise, Respect

For those teachers who "light up the lives of their students," a note of appreciation and a candle for their classroom is an authentic and appreciated award. It can add to the ambiance of the classroom. Many stores will donate the candles for this award. Try Wal-Mart and Target, as they are great supporters of education (Connors, 2000).

Needed: *candles*

Date Used: _____Recipient: _____

MAKE THAT CALL

Praise, Respect, Thanks

This is one of my favorite ways to recognize the efforts of my staff. It has a big payoff and anyone in a leadership role can do it.

On a weekend or during the evening, call your staff and tell them just how much you appreciate their efforts and dedication. Give specific examples of what they have done to deserve your appreciation. Making that call to a staff member's home can be much appreciated, particularly when a staff member is going through times that you or they don't want to discuss at work. Your discreet support will be noted and appreciated.

NOTE: Be aware of the hour. You don't want to call during dinner time.

Date Used: _____Recipient: _____

ME BAG

Respect

This is an activity to bring your group closer together.

Take the time to conduct this icebreaker activity at the beginning of the school year—it can be riveting. Basically, staff members bring in bags with three to five items from home that they feel introduce them completely. Everyone must participate and everyone must be given time to prepare. One teacher at a time brings the items out of the bag and describes how the items represent him or her as a person or as a teacher. A time limit needs to be set for the presentation. Everyone needs enough time to present the contents of his or her bag. If the activity will take more than a day, a random drawing of time slots should occur. Staff members will learn so much about their colleagues through this experience. (Connors, 2000)

NOTE: If staff members forget to bring items, don't have them opt out. You can have them rummage in the office and in their classrooms for items that represent them.

Date Used: _____Recipient: _____

MEETING AGENDAS

Praise, Respect, Thanks

When you put together your staff meeting agendas, you can easily incorporate this idea. Add kudos and acknowledgments to staff members by adding their accomplishments as a header to the form. You can also recognize birthdays or academic and sports accomplishments. See Figure 4.4 for an example of how you can work recognition into your agendas.

Needed: *information to include*

Date Used: _____Recipient: _____

NO FOOD, NO MEETING

Thanks, Respect

Don't hold a meeting without some type of food. It doesn't have to be a large elaborate spread, it just has to say "I care." Chocolate is always a good bet. I've used a box of Tootsie Pops with good results.

Needed: *food*

NOTE: If you have diabetic staff members, you need to have a snack for them as well. It'll pay big dividends if you make an extra effort to include them in the offerings.

Date Used: _____Recipient: _____

FIGURE 4.4
Meeting Agenda

AGENDA
STAFF MEETING

Congratulations to Coach Howard. Her basketball team captured the section title last night. Way to go, Coach!!

1. Change in bus arrival times.

2. Discussion regarding upcoming benchmark assessments.

3. We need dance chaperones for Friday.

Thank you to Brad and Jean for stepping up and chaperoning our recent third grade field trip.

4. Curriculum Share—Fred, you're on.

5. All Star student nominations needed.

6. etc.

7. etc.

Are you looking for some great bulletin board ideas? See Sandy; she has some great ideas and is willing to share.

NO INTERRUPTIONS

Respect

A rather subtle way to recognize the importance of teachers is to avoid interruptions during instruction times. By keeping announcements and interruptions to a minimum, you send a very powerful message that what is going on in class is the most important thing happening on campus.

Date Used: _____Recipient: _____

PERK UP

Thanks

It's simple, but it'll be appreciated.

Bring the person or people on morning duty (supervising children on the playground or getting off the buses) a cup of coffee or hot chocolate. You can buy fancy coffees or just bring some from the staff room. It'll warm their hands and maybe their hearts.

Needed: *hot beverages, cups*

NOTE: You need to know your staff. It won't be appreciated if you bring coffee to someone who doesn't drink coffee.

Date Used: _____Recipient: _____

PIZZA, ANYONE?

Thanks

Have a pizza delivered to the classroom for an employee to thank him or her or to recognize his or her efforts. The students will undoubtedly ask what the pizza is for, so the staff member will be recognized semi-publicly.

Needed: *phone number of a local pizza parlor*

Date Used: _____Recipient: _____

PLAN A STAFF FIELD TRIP

Opportunity, Respect

Instead of having a regular staff meeting, take your staff on a bus ride so that they can see the route their students take to school. Your staff will develop a new understanding of where their students come from, and they will experience the reality of a school bus ride. This activity should be followed by a group lunch (Connors, 2000). You may not have time to do all of the routes, but even traveling some of them could be an eye opener for the staff.

> *"The trip made me think about what is really important. Some of my students are struggling just to survive. I mean, some of them have nothing, not even parents really. It makes me re-think my insistence on getting the homework in. Thanks for taking us. It was an eye opener."*   Jackie, 10th grade math teacher

By taking the teachers and staff on a bus ride around the school district you can make a real impact without saying much. There are always pockets of poverty and violence that our staff doesn't know about or don't want to know about. A simple tour can change a staff.

You can extend this idea by taking a tour of the biggest employer or employers in your area. We went to a lumber mill and saw how they took trees and turned the wood into window and door casements. By seeing where a lot of the students' parents work and where many of the students will work, the teachers have a better sense of the kids and their futures.

> *"This trip to the mill was one of the best staff development activities we have ever had. I can now integrate that environment into my lessons. For instance, you could show students how welders use algebra when repairing equipment at Sierra Pacific. I would love to take my class so that they could job shadow the journeymen. They could show them how they use the math they are learning in high school to perform everyday activities in their jobs."*   Helen, 9th grade math teacher

NOTE: Work with the bus driver. The driver can usually give some additional information on certain areas and students.

Date Used: _____ Recipient: _____

PLANNING DAYS

Opportunity, Respect

This idea will cost the district some money, but can give great payoff in staff morale.

A way to show the teachers that what they do is important is to allow them to have a day or two to do planning for a lesson, activity, or project. Hire a substitute and let the teacher have the time to work on-site planning and gathering materials. This is an addition to district scheduled planning days.

Needed: *substitute teachers*

Date Used: _____ Recipient: _____

POTLUCK

Thanks

Hold quarterly potluck lunches in coordination with staff meetings. It makes both the routine lunch and the boring meeting a lot more bearable. You might even find your staff smiling. Make sure you have staff members sign up for specific types of dishes so you don't end up with all desserts. (Is that a bad thing?)

Date Used: _____Recipient: _____

REPORT CARD REWARD

Praise

Give this idea a try. It's quick and easy, and any leader can use this method of recognition.

Recognize the employees whose children achieve straight *A*s on their report cards. This accomplishment is generally the result of more than just the child's effort—it's rather the effort of both the child and the parents. See Figure 4.5 for a possible letter you can send to your employee.

Date Used: _____Recipient: _____

FIGURE 4.5
Report Card Reward

APPLE SCHOOL DISTRICT
P.O. Box 687, 11918 Main Street, Anytown, CA

Mr. Bill Souza
20201 Gazelle Rd.
Anytown, CA

Dear Mr. Souza:

Please accept my congratulations on Emma's achievement of straight As this reporting period. The achievement shows great effort, dedication, and preparedness on her part. Those qualities will serve her well in the future, but I know that she didn't achieve this distinction alone. You played a significant part as well. Your support, prodding, and continued advocacy for a good education make a great difference. This report card is a positive reflection not only on her, but also on the kind of home environment and guidance you have given.

Again, congratulations on this achievement. It is a pleasure to have such great young people in our district schools as well as to have you represent us every day as a terrific role model and instructional aide.

Respectfully,

RESERVED PARKING

Praise, Thanks

Put up a sign for the Employee of the Month and designate a parking space. It should be the best spot in the lot. It's a small thing, but appreciated, particularly on rainy days.

Needed: *a weatherproof sign*

Date Used: _____Recipient: _____

SAY CHEESE

Praise, Thanks

Take a photo of the person being congratulated for whatever reason. Frame the picture, include a written description of why they were honored, and post the picture in the school office. It will be seen by staff, students, and parents, continuing the recognition long after the actual presentation.

Needed: *camera, bulletin board*

Date Used: _____Recipient: _____

SEND THEM AWAY

Opportunity, Respect

Send your staff or allow staff members to attend conferences or trainings. This sends the message that you view them as professionals and that they are worth the expenditure of funds. Make sure they have business cards of their own to pass out at the conferences. It is always better to send two people to a conference rather than just one. Sending a team of two or more allows them to cover more elements of a conference and it provides them with someone to talk to about the conference and its presentations. Remember, adults speaking about what they learn leads to better comprehension and implementation of new ideas. A way to incorporate this into the area of reward beyond treating them as a professional is to let the lead person choose with whom they wish to travel.

NOTE: Keep a record of who you have sent to trainings or conferences. This will keep you from sending the same people over and over.

Date Used: _____Recipient: _____

SPREAD RUMORS

Praise

When you hear a positive remark about a staff member, repeat it to that person as soon as possible. *"Jerry's mother told me that you are his favorite teacher and that he is learning more from you than from any other teacher."* This is easy to do, and I guarantee you'll get a smile. That small moment will be welcomed and remembered.

Date Used: _____Recipient: _____

SPREAD THE NEWS

Praise

Schools often get letters from parents or grandparents thanking the staff for something they have done that improved the life of their child. A nice way to share these kind words is by reprinting them in your staff newsletter or bulletin (Nelson, 1994).

Needed: *newsletter*

Date Used: _____Recipient: _____

STAND UP

Praise, Thanks

Here's another way to acknowledge the efforts of a staff member without spending a dime.

At the next staff meeting, have everyone stand and give the "honoree" a standing ovation when he or she comes in the door. You can get someone to distract the honoree so that he or she is the last one to arrive at the meeting. It's silly and it will probably redden the cheeks of the honoree, but we all deserve a standing ovation at least once in our lives.

Date Used: _____Recipient: _____

SUPERINTENDENT VISIT

Praise, Respect, Thanks

Ask the superintendent to visit the "targeted" teacher or staff member in his or her classroom and to thank the teacher, in front of the class, for the good job he or she is doing. It will both reward that person and send a powerful message to the students that they have an outstanding teacher or aide. Strangely, this knowledge alone can improve student achievement.

"Whenever you have a superintendent, assistant superintendent, or director in the building, use their presence to your advantage. Share the accomplishments of your faculty with the superintendent while the staff members are present. Make this exchange of information brief, but sincere. The superior will appreciate the knowledge and the staff member will feel great" (Whitaker, Whitaker, & Lumpa, 2000, p. 109).

Date Used: _____Recipient: _____

SWEET TREATS

Praise, Thanks

A little sweetness is a simple and appreciated way to say thanks for all of the things your staff does for their students. Just attach a note to any of these sweet treats.

3 Musketeers: "We're in this together." "One for all, all for one."

M & M's: "Thanks for being a sweet and well-rounded teacher!" or "You're Marvelous and Magnificent."

Almond Joy: "You're a JOY to have on staff," or "You bring JOY and wonder to all of your children. Thank you." or "It's no secret. Working with you is a real JOY."

Payday: "You deserve an extra PAYDAY" or "On this special day, I'd like to let you know I notice the extra things you do for kids. Thank you."

Extra Gum: "You are EXTRA special" or "Thanks for always being willing to do EXTRA" or "Thanks for going that EXTRA mile. It's appreciated."

Mounds: "We appreciate the MOUNDS of work you do!"

Treasure candies: "You are a TREASURE."

Fast Break: "You deserve a BREAK today. Thanks for your hard work."

Pop Rocks: "You ROCK!"

100 Grand bars: "You are worth more than a 100 GRAND to us."

Snickers: "Thanks for all of the laughs" or "Thanks for keeping the mood light" or "I hope you won't SNICKER when I tell you how much your dedication means to me."

Carefree Gum: "Hope your vacation is CAREFREE" or "I don't have a care when I know a child is in your class."

Symphony: "Working together makes a sweet SYMPHONY."

Ding Dongs: "Thanks for working so well with us DING DONGS."

Hershey's Hugs and Kisses: "We love you XOXO"

Cracker Jacks: "You did a Cracker Jack job. Thank you!"

Animal Crackers: "Sometimes it can be a real zoo around here! Thanks for your extra effort!"

Banana Candy: "I went 'ape' over your fantastic presentation. Way to go."

Bubble Gum: "After watching you in action, I'm really stuck on your style."

Butterfinger Bar: "When it comes to being an educator, you never drop the ball."

Chocolate anything: "Just 'choc' up another great year."

Chocolate Eggs: "You're an 'egg-straordinary, egg-spert' educator!"

Crackers: "It's impossible to feel down with a friend like you cracking me up. Thanks for keeping my spirits up."

Crunch Bar: "Thanks for your help. You always come through in the CRUNCH!"

Fifth Avenue Bar: "Your teaching style is really classy."

Fire Stix or Hot Candy: "Your classroom was all fired up with enthusiasm for learning. Thank you for being a fire-starter."

Fruit Roll-Ups: "Roll out the red carpet. You did an amazing job. Thanks!"

Gummy Bears: "You're 'BEARY' special to our school. Thanks for all you do."

Lifesavers: "Thanks. You were a real LIFESAVER."

Mars Bar: "I could look all over the world and not find a teacher as dedicated as you. Thanks! You're truly out of this world."

Mr. Goodbar: "I had to let you know how I feel about you, so here goes, 'You're real good!'"

Orange Slices: "No matter how you slice it, I'll always remember your outstanding effort!"

Peach Candy: "You're PEACHY keen! Thanks for the fine work you do."

Peanuts: I'm nuts about the way you conducted that parent conference yesterday."

Raisins: "Congratulations on 'RAISIN' your test scores. I knew you could do it."

Strawberry Candy: "You're one of the 'berry best."

Sucker: "I'm a real SUCKER for teachers who show kids they care!"

"You saved me! My dog got sick on my shoes this morning; I broke up a fight on the playground this morning and one of the kids stepped on my foot; my students obviously weren't ready for their presentations today and I didn't have a backup plan. The day was just crappy until I found your treat in my mailbox. I really needed and appreciated your gesture and words of encouragement. It made my day."
Marie, 3rd grade teacher

You never really know what your staff is going through on any given day. You may think that a bit of chocolate and a few words won't make much of a difference, but acknowledging someone's contribution always makes a difference.

Needed: *candy, card stock for notes*

Date Used: _____ Recipient: _____

TELL US WHAT YOU THINK

Praise, Thanks

Many times parents have nice things to say about and to our staff, but they don't take the time or have the chance to express their thoughts. You can provide that opportunity by having a book in your main office in which the parents can write notes of appreciation. It doesn't have to be elaborate, just something like a sign-in book at a reception or individual sheets set up for that purpose (see Figure 4.6). Encourage parents to write a few thoughts while they wait for their children to come to the office to go to an appointment. Put it right by the sign-out sheet. Give the notes to the appropriate staff member or read them out loud at your staff meetings if the notes are for the entire staff.

> *"Thank you for taking such good care of my son."*
> Edna, mother of 6th grade student

> *"Dr. Houck, you have made this school into a place where students come first. Your leadership is the reason why BMS has a waiting list. Thank you."* Joanna, parent

On the counter by the student sign-out sheets lies a clipboard with simple thank-you forms for the parents to fill out while they wait for their children to come to the office. It's purely optional, but I have found that parents have good feelings towards the school staff and its programs and want to say "thank you," but like everyone they are busy and rarely get to it. The forms provide a vehicle, and I've always gotten positive feedback to share with my staff.

This is a note we got from a parent who had to move and was withdrawing her child from the school.

I wanted to let you know that I will be mailing back the books for André and Angel, as well as the homework for the both of them and Autumn. I will be sending these items on 12/5/11.

Please let their teachers know, we will miss all staff. The experience at Fort Jones School has been nothing short of memorable. I can't express enough to all of you what a positive effect you have had on us as a family and our children, as students as well as individuals! You are exceptional people that go above and beyond your duties as educators, I am blessed to have had the short amount of time with you, no matter how short. It will last us a life time! God bless all of you. May good things come to each and every one of you. We will keep in touch and hope that you (all) will do the same! André was so elated to receive all the get well cards from his classmates and Mrs. G! He will write them all soon! It's not every day you find people, and in a school no less, that are of your character, caliber, and quality. You will be truly missed!

> *Love Always,*
>
> *Christina, Michael, & Family*

Don't you think this kind of message is worth sharing?
Needed: *pre-printed sheets to display on the counter*

Date Used: _____Recipient: _____

FIGURE 4.6
Tell Us What You Think

❋ THANK YOU ❋ THANK YOU ❋ THANK YOU ❋

Dear (staff member)_____

THANK YOU FOR YOUR EFFORTS.
YOU HAVE MADE A DIFFERENCE TO MY CHILD OR FAMILY BY

_____

_____

_____

_____

_____

_____

_____

My child is _____

❊ *Thanks* ❊

Signature _____

Date _____

THANK THE FAMILY

Praise, Thanks

Send a letter to the family of teachers or coaches, thanking them for their support. Teaching and coaching take a lot of time, and the coaches' families make sacrifices to allow the employee to touch the lives of their students or players. (See Figure 4.7.)

You can also reach out to the families by simply taking the time to call the staff member's spouse or partner and express your appreciation for their willingness to share the staff member with the students.

Needed: *letterhead paper*

Date Used: _____Recipient: _____

THANK THE PARENTS

Praise, Thanks

This is my number one all time favorite. You'll be glad you took the time to do this, and you won't believe the heartfelt responses you'll get.

Send a letter to the parents of your teachers thanking them for supporting the teacher's decision to teach. To get address information, ask for it in the first day packets along with emergency information. See an example in Figure 4.8. This recognition method is the one with which I have had the most impact. You will create happy tears and hugs of appreciation. Every time I have sent this letter out to the parents of my teachers I have received several notes back from the parents with great appreciation of my effort and with pride for their child the teacher.

This is my number one favorite recognition activity. This simple letter has been received by a hundred or so parents and

FIGURE 4.7

Thank the Family

BALLROOM SCHOOL DISTRICT

Anytown, CA
Dr. Ginger Rogers, Superintendent

Dear Howard Family:

I want to thank you for all of the support and patience you have given to your father/husband, Tom, *and* to us as he works for the Ballroom School District. The work that he does is extremely important not only to his students, but also to the community and ultimately the world. I know your father/husband spends a lot of his time at school supporting our activities when you would rather that he be home with you. Please accept our thanks for your sacrifice and know that the district will try to only keep him at school when it is necessary.

Tom does important work, and your support helps make it possible. On behalf of his students and the community, I thank you very much. He couldn't do it without you, and we would not be the district/school we are without him.

Sincerely,

Ginger Rogers

FIGURE 4.8
Thank the Parents

UNIFIED SCHOOL DISTRICT

P.O. Box 687, 11918 Main Street, Anywhere, CA

Mr. Joe Andrieis
2325 Hillside Dr.
Anytown, CA

Dear Mr. Andrieis,

THANK YOU!

I am extending my thanks to you for your contribution to the future of kids. You have raised and encouraged a terrific teacher. Madeleine is one of our finest teachers and a wonderful role model for students. Every day she comes to school eager to share and to learn. I know parents influence their children; I just wanted to acknowledge your part in supporting her and her decision to teach. The curiosity and giving nature that you instilled in her is a gift she is passing on to her students. Thank you for the effort you have put forth and for sharing her with our students and with us. The dedication and time that you and your daughter have committed is changing the world, one student at a time. The Unified School District is a better place because of her contributions.

Sincerely,

I'm always amazed at the response. One crusty old teacher of mine came up to me and hugged me when his parents got the letter. He said his parents framed the letter and put it up on the wall. He was moved to tears, and I was too.

Here are some other responses I've received:

"Bless your heart! We just received your letter about our son Jed and we were so pleased. We have always been proud of him, but to hear it from the superintendent is beyond words. Thank you for taking the time out of your busy day to write to us. It made our year." Parent of a kindergarten teacher

"My mother put hers in her scrapbook."

Susan, 3rd grade teacher

"My parents really liked the letter and mention it all the time. They have shown it off time and again to visitors."

Ellen, 5th grade teacher

Needed: *letterhead paper*

Date Used: _____Recipient: _____

THANKS A LOTTERY

Thanks

Have lottery scratch–off tickets handy to give out as spontaneous recognition or rewards. Verbalize your appreciation when you hand out a ticket. *"Thanks a lottery for what you are doing. You are making a difference."*

Needed: *lottery tickets*

Date Used: _____Recipient: _____

THERE'S MORE TO SCHOOLS
THAN JUST TEACHERS

Opportunity, Respect

When you hold your annual career days for the students, include your classified employees in the presentations. Students should know that it is okay to aspire to jobs in schools other than that of a teacher. Having the cooks, bus drivers, clerks, and secretaries make presentations validates what they do and educates our students.

NOTE: Not all employees will be comfortable with making presentations. Make sure this is an honor and not a burden.

Date Used: _____Recipient: _____

THE UNEXPECTED

Praise

Sometimes you just have to have fun.

Run into a teacher's classroom during class, or into a staff member's work space, and throw confetti and streamers onto the staff member. Sound horns and offer tasty treats. Be silly—it's good for you and the honoree (Connors, 2000). During your romp through their space make sure you describe their recognizable action. "Thank you for completing that report. You're great!" Now, I know many of you are thinking, "I could never do that," but I loved doing this one for my staff while I was a principal. It's okay to have the kids see you being a little nuts.

Needed: *You have to be comfortable being a little crazy.*

Date Used: _____Recipient: _____

WALL OF FAME

Respect

Promote the display of diplomas, certificates, and awards in the teachers' classrooms or on a "Wall of Fame" in the building. We are the only business that keeps our certificates, diplomas, and awards hidden. Encourage the staff to let the students and parents know they are worthy of respect by displaying their awards and credentials. (Connors, 2000)

Date Used: _____Recipient: _____

WAL-MART CHEER

Praise

Wal-Mart employees start each shift with a mini-rally that includes a group cheer. The same format can be used with your staff to enforce the idea of "worthwhile work."

Send an "invitation" to each and every staff member to meet you somewhere visible at a specific time and date. (If you have a very large staff, you might include just the teachers.) It needs to be in the morning before school actually begins. When everyone is present, have them huddle up.

Talk to them about what they do, and tell them that they have the most important job on earth. They make a difference every day, and what they say and do every minute could affect the future of a child. Have everyone put their hands in and give a school cheer. GO TEAM!!

This is a unifying activity that will have your staff wondering about your sanity, but it's valuable to remind them of the importance of their actions. Do this in an area where the students will see the event. It will start the kids talking, and they will ask their teachers what it was all about. The teachers verbalize the importance of the activity to the students, and it will reinforce the concept. I suggest doing this four or five times a year.

Date Used: _____Recipient: _____

WELCOME THEM

Opportunity, Respect

This simple gesture has been received well at my schools. It works for superintendents, principals, union presidents, PTA leaders, or department heads.

The day before a new employee comes to work, have several current employees call the employee and welcome him or her to the school. Remember that we lose many of our fine new teachers because they don't feel supported or connected in their job. This simple call can start their experience on a positive note (Nelson, 1994). **Needed:** *phone numbers of the new employees*

Date Used: _____Recipient: _____

WORKING IN YOUR PAJAMAS

Opportunity, Respect

When you have an employee come to you with a new idea or with a request to do some planning, allow the staff member to work on the project from home rather than at school. This demonstrates trust of your employees, because you are treating them as professionals. They'll probably get more done because there will likely be fewer interruptions at home.

Date Used: _____Recipient: _____

YOU'RE APPRECIATED NOTES

Praise, Thanks

Have a stack of the "You Are Appreciated" forms in your staff room so that everyone can send the notes to their peers. Duplicate a simple form on a half or quarter sheet of NCR paper. Deliver one copy to the appreciated person and display one on a bulletin board to share the kindness with the whole school. See Figure 4.9 for an example.

"Even though people say nice things to you, it means something more when people take the time to write their name on a piece of paper and say it" (Nelson, 1994). When you walk into the staff room at our school the first thing you see is the bulletin board filled with "You're Appreciated" note cards. It sets such a positive tone for the whole school, and it's difficult not to go over and read the sentiments. This is a note I got back just because I acknowledged someone's efforts.

"What a nice surprise to find your note in my mailbox today. It means a lot to be noticed and appreciated. Thank you for taking the time and for your kind remarks."

Teri, Title 1 teacher

I find advertising positive efforts and achievements breeds more positive effort.

Needed: *pre-printed NCR quarter sheets*

Date Used: _____Recipient: _____

FIGURE 4.9
You're Appreciated

YOU ARE APPRECIATED

_____

[Recipient name]

Thank you for

_____

_____

_____

_____

_____

_____

_____   _____

Signed   Date

~ 5 ~

Moderate-Effort Ideas

Moderate-Effort Ideas

Item	Page	Thanks	Praise	Respect	Opportunity
A Visit from the Past	69	x	x	x	
Aahhh	71	x			
An Apple a Day	71	x	x	x	
Ask Their Opinion	72			x	x
Be Graphic	73	x	x	x	
Break the Routine	74			x	x
Brown Bag It	74	x			
Bus Drivers Rock	75	x	x	x	
Crosswords	75		x	x	
Decorate the Lounge	76	x		x	
Don't Forget the Subs	76			x	
Duty Calls	77	x		x	
Feature Them	78	x	x	x	
Friday Focus	78	x	x	x	
Getting Pinned	84	x		x	
Give Flowers	84	x	x		
Happy Holidays	85	x	x	x	
Immediate Feedback	87		x	x	x
Mentoring Programs	90				x
Midterm Break	90	x			
Military Families	91	x		x	
Open Your House	92	x		x	
Place Mats	92	x	x	x	
Pride Wall	94		x		
Put Their Name in Lights	94	x	x		
Recognizing Expertise	95			x	x

Item	Page	Thanks	Praise	Respect	Opportunity
Room Service	96	x			
Shadow a Teacher	97			x	x
Spread the Word	97	x	x	x	
Stressed/Desserts	98	x			
Survival Kit	99			x	
Table Topper	99		x	x	
Take an Ad	100	x	x		
Team Lunch	101			x	x
Tell the Boss	101	x	x	x	
Tell the Story in Pictures	101		x	x	
While They Play	102	x		x	
Whine and Cheese Party	102	x			
Wingspread Award	103		x	x	
You Are	104	x	x	x	

A VISIT FROM THE PAST

Praise, Thanks, Respect

When I was teaching, nothing made my day any brighter than having former students stop by and share what was going on in their lives. The fact that they took time out of their day to remember me was sustaining. A "Visit from the Past" builds on that idea. Too many times we in education don't see the impact we have made on our students and on our world. A way to bring this home and to show your staff how much what they do really matters is to invite former students back to the school for a visit. This can be done on an informal basis by having them come by any time they can, or you can set up a specific day for visits. You could incorporate it into your homecoming events if you are a high school. Put an ad in the local paper asking for alumni to stop by for a visit. Let them know that the purpose of the event is to show teachers that they had an influence on their students' lives, that what teachers do is important, and that they are appreciated. You'll be pleased by the response, and the staff will appreciate your efforts and feel good about what they do.

Imagine that you are a teacher, and you enter the school gym or cafeteria, which is filled with soft music and pictures on the walls of students and classes from the past. You see finger foods on the table and know that there are no expectations of you other than to have a good time and enjoy the afternoon.

The event is aligned with the high school homecoming events, and many of your former colleagues and students are in attendance. People with familiar faces approach you and share with you that you made a difference in their lives. It's because of your science lesson on anatomy that Susan became a doctor. Sheldon is anxious for you to meet his wife, saying that you were his favorite teacher.

The first time we offered this event, we had about 60 former students and teachers attend. Everyone had a good time and there was lots of hugging and laughter. It helped that we provided name tags so the teachers didn't have to guess at who the guests were. These are some of the responses from former students:

"Ms. H. I often think about those people who have had a positive influence in my life and you are definitely one of those. Your words back then made little sense, but with the years of life and the experiences we go through, they make sense now, and I am grateful for the guidance."

Jose, taken from a "Visit from the Past" sign-in book.

"You know, I am in my tenth year of teaching and fourth year as an assistant principal. It amazes me that the experiences I had all those years ago on the field really shaped the person and teacher I am today. You have no idea how much influence you had. I learned how to work hard, but also to laugh and enjoy the moment."

Jessamy, commenting as a former softball player.

"I have to tell you that you were such a positive influence in my life and I really appreciate(d) you. My parents weren't the best role models and you were always positive. Thank you."

Tami, former student

Date Used: _____Recipient: _____

AAHHH!!

Thanks

This one will cost you a little bit, but it will make you a hero.

Hire a massage therapist who has a chair and will come to your school. Pay her or him for the whole day and encourage your staff to come in and get a massage on their prep time. Chair massages are not as personally intrusive as a full massage and can be done in the staff room. Your staff will purrrrr.

Needed: *A massage therapist*

Date Used: _____Recipient: _____

AN APPLE A DAY

Praise, Thanks, Respect

This is a thank-you that is good for more than the soul.

- Place an apple on every teacher's desk or in their mailbox with a note that says "an apple a day keeps stress away" (Connors, 2000).
- Have your student council polish apples and place them on a silver platter with a silver cover. The students go into the teacher's classroom dressed up in formal wear, carrying the tray and serve each teacher an apple (Margie Cummings, Ridgefield H.S., www.wacaonline.org/resources_staff.html).
- Greet each teacher as they come onto campus and present them with a freshly polished apple. Wish them a good day and thank them for their effort in improving the lives of children.

Needed: *apples, serving tray*

Date Used: _____Recipient: _____

ASK THEIR OPINION

Opportunity, Respect

Asking staff their opinion validates them as professionals with something to contribute.

- Privately asking teachers or staff for their opinion about how things are going on campus or how you should proceed with a project is a powerful way to recognize a person. If staff members know you respect their opinion and that they can be part of a solution, it will energize them in a much greater way than any gift could.
- Involve your staff in interviewing and hiring of new staff. They can read resumes, sit on interview panels, or do informal hospitality interviews.
- Rotate the responsibility of running the regular staff meetings among your teachers.
- Have enough meaningful committees that everyone sits on a committee, but only one. This involves everyone, but keeps the responsibility level equal.

"If you trust your employees with your organization's most valuable assets, why not trust them to use their judgment" (Yerkes, 2001, p. 11).

Needed: *List of employees divided by job classification. Mark off their names as you meet with them or use them on a committee or in the hiring process. This will allow you to include everyone.*

Date Used: _____Recipient: _____

BE GRAPHIC

Praise, Thanks, Respect

Give the staff graphic reminders of their continuing efforts or of their progress and success on any given goal. Just as you display those big thermometers when you are raising money, create charts that outline student positions on benchmarks or state-mandated test results as a visual reminder of what it would take to move a student into another performance band. Use a poster maker, or do it by hand, and create a line graph depicting your school's/district's assessment journey. Every time your staff sees these charts they will be reminded of their success and of the task at hand. See Figure 5.1.

Needed: *Some sort of graphic display.*

Date Used: _____Recipient: _____

FIGURE 5.1
Be Graphic

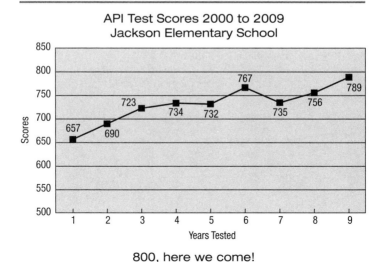

API Test Scores 2000 to 2009
Jackson Elementary School

800, here we come!

BREAK THE ROUTINE

Opportunity, Respect

A change in scenery can be a way to encourage innovative thinking. Doing this before tackling a big project can start it off right.

An easy way to do this is to hold some of your staff meetings off campus, maybe at a home or in a restaurant. You might even try a park and enjoy the sunshine. Breaking that "same old thing" routine can energize thinking.

Needed: *Transportation*

Date Used: _____Recipient: _____

BROWN BAG IT

Thanks

Bring the deserving person bagged lunches for a week, making sure you include dessert. A nice extra is to decorate the bag with things that represent the honored person (Nelson, 1994). Don't forget to add an appreciative note inside or on the outside of the bag.

Needed: *decorated brown bag, lunch*

NOTE: You might ask about the staff member's favorite foods and allergies.

Date Used: _____Recipient: _____

BUS DRIVERS ROCK

Praise, Respect, Thanks

Sometimes we overlook our hardworking bus drivers. Here are some ways to let them feel appreciated.

- Invite the bus drivers into school for lunch.
- Have the principals or superintendent ride the bus route with the drivers so they can have an appreciation for the job the drivers do every day.
- Include their pictures on your staff picture bulletin board.
- Present certificates of appreciation to them at board meetings.

Date Used: _____ Recipient: _____

CROSSWORDS

Praise, Respect

This is a fun way to spread the word and acknowledge people without a lot of fanfare.

Acknowledge employees' contributions or accomplishments by integrating their deeds into a crossword puzzle published in the district or school newsletter. The district puzzle also may, hopefully, give others some ideas that they can try in their classrooms or at their schools.

You can give out a prize for the first person or group that finishes the puzzle. Try it as a handout at your staff development meeting or staff meeting. It'll get people talking to each other. An example of items you could incorporate, "12 down—teacher that celebrated Pi Day on March 14 (3.14) with activities investigating pi with edible round things."

Needed: *You could create the puzzle from scratch, but I suggest you find some software to help you create it.*

NOTE: This can be done several times during the year.

Date Used: _____Recipient: _____

DECORATE THE LOUNGE

Thanks, Respect

Are you looking for ideas that the student council can help with? Here you go.

Enlist the students to decorate the teachers' lounge with banners and signs that demonstrate that the students appreciate the efforts the teachers make every day (Connors, 2000). Don't leave them up permanently—they'll lose their impact.

Needed: *craft paper, scissors, markers or paint, glue, tape*

Date Used: _____Recipient: _____

DON'T FORGET THE SUBS

Respect

Have pre-made baskets ready for the first time a sub comes to your school. Include chocolate, an invitation to join the staff for lunch, a school pen, and any other items you might wish to include. Put them together in a basket and have them ready for the subs to take. It'll make them feel wanted and do a good deal for your school's public relations.

"I like working here. You don't make me feel like a stranger."
Helen, substitute teacher

"Thank you for the wonderful welcome basket. This district is my favorite to work in. You make an effort to make subs a part of the team. At other schools you don't even feel welcome in the lunch room." Maria, substitute teacher

Our welcome baskets include such things as a school T-shirt, pads of hall passes, school pens, chocolate, and a school mug. We give this to every substitute teacher the first time they work in our school. We have had great success. We don't pay as much as the neighboring districts, but we have no trouble getting subs to come work for us.

"I don't sub anymore, but I still have my T-shirt!" Jack

Needed: *school pen, school T-shirt, chocolate, sticky notes, basket*

Date Used: _____Recipient: _____

DUTY CALLS

Thanks, Respect

I was thinking of principals when I wrote this one, but superintendents, department heads, and classified managers certainly could do this.

It'll mean a lot to a person not have to stand in the cold on a winter morning. Hand the person a coffee and tell them that they have given to the cause, now it's repayment time. You, the administrator, standing morning duty, or any duty, will be appreciated not only by the person you relieve, but it will send a positive message to other staff members that observe you doing this routine duty.

Needed: *A staff duty assignment list*

Date Used: _____Recipient: _____

FEATURE THEM

Praise, Respect, Thanks

Do you publish a newsletter? Here's an idea to incorporate.

Feature the chosen person in your newsletters that go to parents or staff. Include personal information about the employee such as family, hobbies, and special talents. You can make things a little more interesting by asking some nontraditional questions, such as, "What type of vegetable do you associate the most with your personality?" or "If you could be any animal in the world what would you be and why?" These might not be typical interview questions, but they will catch people's attention.

Needed: *newsletter, information about the staff member*

Date Used: _____Recipient: _____

FRIDAY FOCUS

Praise, Respect, Thanks

Communicating your vision and goals are vital to moving any organization forward, but so are the everyday items of school life. Including everyone in your plans sends the message that they are important members of the team. You can't over-communicate with your staff. One "tried and true way" to communicate with your staff and to recognize staff achievement is to send out a weekly wrap-up memo. The memo can be called anything, that isn't important. What is important is to include upcoming activity dates and details, goals for the week's Professional Learning Community (PLC), if you do such things, and kudos to the staff regarding things you have seen or they have done during the week. It's important to put these in the staff's (all staff members, teachers and classified) mailboxes before folks leave on Fridays.

This allows them to have a good sense of the coming week and be prepared for activities happening on Monday. Figures 5.2 and 5.3 show examples of ways the memos can be formatted. Below are some tips suggested by Whitaker and others in *Motivating and Inspiring Teachers* (Whitaker, Whitaker, & Lumpa, 2000).

1. Create an attractive format and use it consistently.
2. Use colored paper. Choose a color at the start of the school year and use it each week; don't use this color for anything else. Make it special.
3. Make sure the newsletter is in staff mailboxes at the same time each week. People will look forward to and expect your memo.
4. Post the current Friday Focus in the teacher's lounge. This allows for quick reference for those who misplace their copy.
5. Collect quotes, inspirational thoughts, and cartoons. This will keep you from having to scramble at the last minute for your weekly thought.
6. Make notes of events you see when you are "out and about." This can come in handy when you are writing your memo. The more personal items the better. Use staff names.
7. In your planner, keep a running list of items that you want to include each week. Jot down notes to yourself throughout the week and you will find that finishing up on Thursday is simple.
8. Include "Friday Focus Featured Folks." You can either write a short article about a staff member or teacher, or you can assign folks to write about themselves.
9. Offer your "quote of the week."
10. Make sure you are upbeat and comfortable when you write the newsletter.
11. Put your heart into it and have fun!

Other items to be included

- Kudos or recognition of staff efforts.
- Have a calendar of the week's events.
- If you have weekly PLCs or collaboration days, state what the goal was last week and what the goal is for the coming week.
- Include staff birthdays if there are any.

"When you hold official meetings, employees should not be surprised by what they hear. If you are doing a good job keeping everyone informed, then people will rally behind you in tough times and celebrate with you in good times" (Podmoroff, 2005, p. 238). Your staff knowing what they are expected to achieve is very motivating. Purpose is a powerful motivator. This goes directly to the need for employees to have control of the goal.

Needed: *time, colored copy paper*

Date Used: _____Recipient: _____

FIGURE 5.2

Monday Memo

MONDAY MEMO

For the week of March 5th

PLC-COLLABORATION

Last week's goal was to complete essential standards for language arts and have a hard copy to department chairman by March 3.

The Week Ahead

Monday
Soccer at Home, 4:00. IEP for H.K., 3:30.

Tuesday
Staff meeting, Rm. 6. See agenda on back.

Wednesday
Soccer Away. PLC—bring your binders.

Thursday
Dance, 6:00, looking for chaperones.

Our goal this week is to start your pacing guides for language arts. They are due March 15.

Friday
Department meetings at lunch.

KUDOS TO:

Helen Herd for use of technology in teaching. She has integrated technology into her lesson in a way that engages the students and hopefully will actually lessen prep time. Well done. See Helen for tips.

Mary Sakuma—Thank you for volunteering to take the students to the recycling center last week. We all appreciate your effort.

Kathy Wheeler for hosting our TGIF. We all needed it. Thank you for opening your home.

A big thank you to all of you for making our Back-to-School Night a rousing success. We had a record breaking 678 parents join us. I received many positive comments about how nice the school looks and how prepared the teachers were. Many of the parents appreciated the video presentations. BRAVO!!

FIGURE 5.3
Friday Fishwrap

The Friday Fishwrap

To: All ESD Employees
From: Superintendent/Principal Mary Sakuma
March 17, 2009

Leprechaun Mischief

Friday! No, Monday! NOOO . . . Tuesday!
A mischievous little leprechaun got hold of the Friday Fishwrap and delayed its delivery until today . . . He also altered the color of the paper usually used for the Fishwrap.
Bad leprechaun!

Science & Art Fair Tonight!

Come out and enjoy an evening of art and science in the Junction Gym. The event starts at 6 p.m. Refreshments will be available for purchase.

Faculty Meetings

There will be a K-8 faculty meeting on Monday, March 23, from 3:15 to 4:15 p.m. Please bring your Tools for Teaching book and your VIP power point, if possible.

● ● ●

Kudos

A big kudos for our maintenance crew who turned "The Swamp" into a 1st class softball field by opening day!

● ● ●

Important Dates

Okay, we have some final-final dates for the spring calendar:

Thursday, March 19	Board meeting
Monday, March 23@ 9 a.m	D.A.R.E. Graduation
Friday, March 27 @ 10 a.m.	E.S. Awards Assembly
Friday, April 3 @ 1:15 p.m.	M.S. Awards Assembly
Tuesday, April 7 @ 6:15 p.m.	8th grade Cake Auction
Friday, April 10	Snow Day
Mon–Fri April 13–17	Spring Break
Monday, April 20	Staff Development (teachers)
Thursday, April 23	Board meeting
Thursday, May 14	Middle School Open House (Incl. 6th & 8th grade Project Night)
Wednesday, May 20	4th to 8th grade Band Concert
Thursday, May 28	Elementary Open House

(Contributed by Mrs. Mary Sakuma)

• • •

Good for a Few Laughs

Sammy had stolen the rabbi's gold watch. He didn't feel too good about it, so he decided, after a sleepless night, to go to the rabbi.

"Rabbi, I stole a gold watch."

"But Sammy! That's forbidden! You should return it immediately!"

"What shall I do?"

"Give it back to the owner."

"Do you want it?"

"No, I said return it to its owner."

"But he doesn't want it."

"In that case, you can keep it."

• • •

GETTING PINNED

Thanks, Respect

A tangible symbol of appreciation for service and longevity is that of recognition pins dedicated to years of service—5, 10, 15 years, etc. This should be done at your opening of school meeting or at a board meeting for both certificated and classified staff members marking their anniversaries. We appreciate the years of service our staff members give the district. The pins will serve as a reminder of that appreciation.

Needed: *service pins*

Date Used: _____ Recipient: _____

GIVE FLOWERS

Praise, Thanks

Any school leader can implement this idea. It can demonstrate caring from any or every level. It's a great way to start out the school year.

On the first day of everyone's employment, have flowers on their desk in the morning. They don't have to come from a florist—taking cuttings out of your yard or getting a bouquet from the grocery store will work. Don't you think that would make a nice first impression of you and your school?

> *"Wow! Thank you so much for the flowers. I've never had a boss make such a gesture. They made me feel very welcome."*
> Joann, high school history teacher

Imagine coming into a new job on your first day. You're anxious, both nervous and excited. You enter your classroom or your work station and there sits a colorful bouquet of flowers on your desk. The note attached reads "Welcome to _____ School. We are very excited to have you join our team."

"No one has ever given me flowers before. Thank you."

Ida, cook

Needed: *flowers*

Date Used: _____Recipient: _____

HAPPY HOLIDAYS

Praise, Thanks, Respect

Another one of my favorites!

Send a holiday card to the spouses, partners, and family members of the staff members. The card should include a picture of the staff member with the children with whom they work. The pictures don't need to be candid shots but should be flattering pictures of the staff member. An example can be seen in Figure 5.4. (Adapted from an idea developed by Whitaker, Whitaker, & Lumpa, 2000.) This idea is one of my favorites and always gets a positive response.

Needed: card stock, a picture of every employee with students, color printer

NOTE: *Be mindful of those staff members who might not celebrate the winter holidays.*

Date Used: _____Recipient: _____

FIGURE 5.4
Happy Holidays

Front of card:

During this holiday time
we'd like to share with you
a valued treasure of the
Rethink School District

Inside of card:

She makes our school
a better place in which to learn.

We wish you a wonderful holiday season.

IMMEDIATE FEEDBACK

Praise, Respect, Opportunity

When you make observations in classrooms it is natural for the teachers to wonder what you thought of their performance. Here are several ways to recognize them and to give them immediate feedback regarding their performance—both casually and formally.

- Even when you drop into classrooms for just a few minutes you can give the teacher feedback on his or her performance without spending a long time on official write-ups. I have used the form shown in Figure 5.5 successfully. You can customize it to meet your needs and the specific goals you have for instructional practices. I print mine two to an 8.5 × 11 page. Leave the form on the teacher's desk or in his or her mailbox.

- Another quick and easy way to give feedback on your drop-in visits is to have a notebook by the door in every classroom. When you come into the class simply get the notebook and jot down a few thoughts. You can ask questions of the teacher by this method as well. Make sure that the book isn't available to the students.

- When you do your official classroom observations, you can provide immediate feedback to ease the teacher's anxiety. Schedule several observations in one day—as many as you can. Hire a substitute for the same day as the observations. As soon as you finish with an observation, invite the teacher back to your office. The substitute takes the teacher's class. Debrief the observation with the teacher and discuss your observations and thoughts. At a later date you can write up the formal document and again go over it with the teacher. By talking about the observations right away you are able to give the teachers immediate feedback, and you can talk about the issues while they are fresh and not days or weeks old. This method is very effective, as many administrators don't always get the write-up done or the follow-up meeting scheduled as soon as they should. This provides some leeway in our busy schedules.

"Thanks for meeting with me now. I'm so nervous; I don't think I would have been much good the rest of the day— worrying. Even my students knew I was nervous."

Mary, 9th grade teacher commenting on being able to discuss her observation immediately afterward and not having to wait days for my feedback

"I appreciate getting the check box notes after a visit from you. The most meaningful notes are ones that have a written comment on them and that they are positive, since the visit is unannounced and I don't get to talk with you about what you saw afterwards. It is nice that you just mention the good parts of the lesson." Erin, resource teacher

"I have saved all of the check box notes you have given me. They are positive. I like the way it begins, 'During my brief visit to your classroom I saw the following quality instructional practices. Keep up the good work.' Twice you have commented on the great rapport I have with students as well as celebrations of success. This is a great tool to remind teachers of what we are doing right." Susan, 5th grade teacher

These are a few of the comments I have gotten when I use immediate feedback techniques. The first one is from a brand new teacher who was terrified during my first observation. By immediately sending in a sub to cover her class while we went over the observation, I was able to calm her, and that allowed her to be more productive the rest of the day.

The checkbox sheets are great for any administrator to use when dropping into a classroom. They're quick, easy to use, and always positive. Teachers appreciate the feedback.

Date Used: _____Recipient: _____

FIGURE 5.5
Immediate Feedback

Teacher _____ Date _____

Lesson _____

During my brief visit to your classroom I saw the following quality instructional practices. Keep up the good work.

☐ Wait time utilized

☐ Random name generation

☐ Proximity teaching

☐ Links to previous learning

☐ Inference questioning

☐ Checking for understanding

☐ Smooth effective transitions

☐ Lesson objective stated

☐ Summarizes main points

☐ Front loading of vocabulary

☐ Contact with *all* students

☐ Appropriate or challenging vocabulary

☐ Efficient distribution of materials

☐ Redirects inappropriate behavior effectively

☐ Use of visuals/graphic organizers

☐ Celebration of success

☐ Dignifies errors

☐ Models solutions

☐ Enthusiasm for lesson

☐ Technology integrated

☐ Real life connection

☐ Clear directions

☐ All students engaged

☐ Differentiated instruction

☐ Student talk time

I came in at the
☐ beginning
☐ middle
☐ end
of the lesson

_____

_____

_____ *Emily*

MENTORING PROGRAMS

Opportunity

Here's an item that can be done at the departmental level, school level, or district level.

This idea doesn't cost a thing, and it can pay big dividends for your school. Assign all new staff members a mentor to introduce them to the culture and traditions of the school. It's nice to have a person they can go to to find out about the daily functions of the school, as well as for information on how to be more effective in their jobs. We lose new teachers from the profession due to stress and isolation. By providing a "go to" person we can reduce our turnover of energetic and dedicated teachers.

Needed: *quality teachers to step forward*

Date Used: _____Recipient: _____

MIDTERM BREAK

Thanks

As the second semester starts, have a halfway party for the staff. Cut all of the food you serve in half. Only serve half cups of coffee, soda, etc. If you have an agenda or card for the staff, cut the copies in half lengthwise so people have to find a partner to match up with to be able to read it. Pass out cards with the name of half of a famous duo, (e.g., Batman & Robin), and have members find their "better halves." If they find this person, award them a candy bar or other prize. Get some area restaurants to donate coupons for "half off" a meal or "buy one get one free" and have a drawing halfway through the meeting.

(http://michiganprincipals.org/masc/staff_appreciation.htm)

Needed: *party supplies cut in half, card stock for famous name cards, rewards*

Date Used: _____Recipient: _____

MILITARY FAMILIES

Respect, Thanks

This project is planned for teachers who are serving in the military and have been called up for active duty. The parents, other teachers, and students can collect useful items to send to them in care packages (for instance: soap, deodorant, sunscreen, snack items, cards, letters, and banners). This allows the schools to do something productive in a worrisome time and, best of all, lets that teacher know that they are supported, missed, and remembered by those at home.

This project can easily be expanded to include the children of teachers or staff members who have been sent "in harm's way." The school could "adopt" a staff member's child and send them items and letters. This would certainly make the staff member feel important and cared for.

Needed: *list of active service personnel, collections of soap, lotion, games, treats, etc.*

NOTE: Be careful about the cost of shipping. It can get out of hand quickly. Consider the PTO or the Booster Club to help defray the costs.

Date Used: _____Recipient: _____

OPEN YOUR HOUSE

Respect, Thanks

Invite your employees to your house for a special celebration or for a casual T.G.I.F. By opening your house, you break down the barriers of "us and them." You don't have to provide an elaborate spread—you can have everyone bring their own drinks and you can pour out a few bags of chips. It's the being together that counts, not the food.

Needed: *snack foods*

Date Used: _____Recipient: _____

PLACEMATS

Praise, Respect, Thanks

Figure 5.6 is an example of a restaurant placemat designed and printed on 11 × 15 paper by the school district in conjunction with a local restaurant. The school district prints them and provides them free to the restaurant. The community loves to come in and read the names, recognizing their children, grandchildren or neighbors. While this doesn't directly honor or recognize the teaching staff it does bring the school and their accomplishments into the public eye. The idea could easily be expanded to be used for recognizing Employees of the Month or for any reason.

Needed: *Information about the employee or the event you wish to publicize, 11 × 15 paper, and a printer that will handle that size paper.*

Date Used: _____Recipient: _____

FIGURE 5.6
Placemats

BOB RANCH HOUSE CONGRATULATES
AND THANKS THESE EDUCATORS

FARMERS SCHOOL DISTRICT RECOGNIZES

The faculty and staff members that have served the students of the
Farmer School District for more than 20 years

Hill High School

Judy Houck
Tabitha Reynolds
Jake Howard
Jakie Lane
Lisa Dean
Anthony Lee
Rhea Leishman
Theda White
Robert Ross
Fred Ginger
Debra DeWitt

Dale Middle School

Jeannie Forrest
Ted Reynolds
Terry Costello
Mary Sakuma
Nancy Silva
Joy Edwards
Todd Whittaker
Chris Forrester
Jeanne Thomas
Helen Herd
Billy High

THANK YOU!!!

PRIDE WALL

Praise

On a wall in the main hallway of your school or in the main office, display a picture of every staff member (you can snip one off their school pictures before they get them). You can post only the teachers, but I recommend displaying everyone. Everyone is important to the success of the school. Next to each picture put a note with the staff member's name, their specific job, and the date they joined the school. You can also include where they went to high school, what college they graduated from, and their major. I have also included their all-time favorite book. (Reading is important.) You'll be amazed at the number of times the students will point out their teacher's picture to their parents or how much attention the display gets from visitors.

Needed: *picture of every employee, information about the employees*

Date Used: _____Recipient: _____

PUT THEIR NAME IN LIGHTS

Praise, Thanks

If your town has a business with an electronic billboard, arrange to have your "Employee of the Month," or for any reason, an employee's name put in lights (Nelson, 1994). This honors your employee and promotes your school or district as a friendly, supportive place.

Needed: *access to a lighted marquee*

Date Used: _____Recipient: _____

RECOGNIZING EXPERTISE

Opportunity, Respect

Here are three quick ways to recognize the expertise of your teachers:

1. A great way to tell a teacher that he or she is doing a good job is to encourage others to do observations in his or her classroom. Whether it is through a structured program, such as having every teacher do an observation within the district, or for those teachers who are struggling or in need of some new ideas, it is a great compliment to direct others to the classroom of those who you think are doing a good job. They may be a bit embarrassed or nervous, but they'll be honored too.

2. When you assign a "difficult" student to a classroom, you can turn the situation into a recognition moment. Verbally point out to the teacher that they were chosen specifically for this student because you believe in them and their talents. You know that they are the best teacher for this particular student and that you know both of them will be successful. Yes, it might be PR, but it can also be true and start a tough situation out positively.

3. Discipline issues are a part of the administrative day, and you can actually use these encounters to motivate and recognize staff members. When you have a student in your office who has disrupted class or who is a frequent visitor to you, try this: Invite the classroom teacher or the other staff member involved into the office with the disruptive student. Use this statement or something like it— "_____, you have continued to disrupt class and waste not only the class's time but your teacher's

time. Your teacher (or aide) is one of the best teachers we have at this school, and your behavior makes me wonder if you deserve to be in her class. If you want to continue to have the best, you need to improve your behavior." This technique was used while I was a classroom teacher and I have never forgotten it. I did appreciate the indirect compliment.

Date Used: _____Recipient: _____

ROOM SERVICE

Thanks

Take a cart of fresh coffee, donuts, and fresh orange juice to staff members throughout the school. It's okay to go in during instruction. The students should see that you appreciate what the teachers do. A white towel over the arm would be a nice touch.

Needed: *breakfast food or afternoon snack food, "silver" serving tray, white towel*

NOTE: You can perform this task or recruit a parent volunteer or student.

Date Used: _____Recipient: _____

SHADOW A TEACHER

Opportunity, Respect

Encourage business leaders, school board members, and parents to shadow a teacher for the day. Send cards and make phone calls to keep encouraging different people to come and visit your school. The more these people see what teachers do on a daily basis, the better they will understand their needs and positions. It's hard to support what they don't know about. Let them see first-hand the ongoing, incredible activities developed by your teachers (Connors, 2000). Additionally, it sends a subtle message to the teacher chosen for this activity. "The principal must think highly of me to be chosen for a visit and to represent our school."

Date Used: _____Recipient: _____

SPREAD THE WORD

Praise, Respect, Thanks

Write and publish a personal ad or publicity article in the local newspaper. Include a picture of the employee or employees you are recognizing. This can be done for an individual or for an accomplishment of the school. See an example of a newspaper ad in Figure 5.7

"There is nothing more fun than the celebration of a success or a shared win. The celebration itself creates energy for ongoing efforts. What gets recognized gets repeated; what gets celebrated becomes a habit" (Yerkes, 2001, p. 11).

Date Used: _____Recipient: _____

FIGURE 5.7
Spread the Word

> ## Congratulations
>
> To all of the students and staff members of the
> Scott Valley Unified School District:
>
> Your hard work has paid off! We raised our Academic Performance Index
> by 25 points and now we are over the 850 mark as a district.
>
> We are the highest scoring school district in the county.
>
> Thank you for your dedication and hard work. Well done.
>
> Dr. Emily Houck,
> Superintendent
>
> *paid for with private funds

*This tells the staff and the public that the ad wasn't paid for with district funds.

STRESSED/DESSERTS

Thanks

Your local PTO/PTA might be willing to help with this one.

Yes, stressed is desserts spelled backwards. Reward your staff with a surprise party of just desserts. This event is especially good at stressful times, such as right before testing. The group should be encouraged to share their stress-reducing techniques. (Connors, 2000)

Needed: *desserts*

NOTE: You might also include some fruit for those who are watching their weight.

Date Used: _____ Recipient: _____

SURVIVAL KIT

Respect

You generally know in the spring that you are going to be hiring a new teacher for the following fall. A nice way to recognize and welcome the new teacher is to have already ordered the needed supplies for the classroom, such as: paperclips, paper, tape, and lesson plan book. The new teacher has enough to do without worrying about where to find these types of items. It would be a nice gesture to include things that will make the teacher part of the team such as: a school T-shirt, school mug, a pack of hall passes, and a supply of chocolate. (Nelson, 1997)

Needed: *office supplies, planning book, school shirt, coffee mug*

Date Used: _____Recipient: _____

TABLE TOPPER

Praise, Respect

The table topper is another idea that can be used to recognize the work of your schools as a whole or to recognize individual accomplishments or activities. The example in Figure 5.8 recognizes the efforts of the entire teaching staff as it relates to mandated state testing, but it could easily be designed to advertise the happenings in a specific classroom throughout the district. This idea works in collaboration with a local restaurant to display the trifold on their tables for a period of time. Simply fold the 8.5" by 11" card stock publication into a three-sided figure, tape or glue the sides together, and stand on a table.

Needed: *card stock, tape, color printer*

Date Used: _____Recipient: _____

FIGURE 5.8

YOU SHOULD BE PROUD!

HOW THE STATE JUDGES SCHOOL PERFORMANCE

WHAT IS THE STAR TESTING PROGRAM?

One part of the state testing system is called the Standardized Testing and Reporting (STAR) program. This program, administrated annually, was authorized in 1997 through Senate Bill 376. The purpose of the STAR program is to help measure how well students in California public schools are learning academic skills and to hold the education community accountable for their progress. These scores are compared nationally.

WHO MUST TAKE THE STAR TEST?

All students in grades 2 through 11 must take the STAR designated test. Students learning English and students in special education programs are included in "all" students, and they must take the test. The only students exempted from the testing are students whose Individual Education Plan (IEP) specially exempt them from standardized testing and students with written parent requests to exempt them.

The Etna Deli supports Valley Schools

YOU SHOULD BE PROUD!

VALLEY SCHOOLS LEAD COUNTY IN ACADEMIC PERFORMANCE INDEX

The Academic Performance Index is a scaled score from 100-1000. All schools in California are to be in the 800s by 2014.

	2008 API
FRANK HIGH SCHOOL	767
JEAN ELEMENTARY	881
JOHN ELEMENTARY	856
MARY JUNIOR HIGH	835
PETE SCHOOL	805

	County average API	State average API
High schools	729	702
Junior highs	791	735
Elementary schools	749	776

The Etna Deli supports Valley Schools

YOU SHOULD BE PROUD!

WHAT HAS LED TO OUR SUCCESS

- **Dedicated and hard working staff, teachers and administrators**
- **Supportive parents**
- **Instructional after-school programs**
- **Fifth grade science camp**
- **Award winning programs**
  History Day project, FHS agriculture program, service learning projects, high school newspaper
- **Award winning schools**
  California Distinguished School, Title 1 Academic Achievement School, Top Ten National High Schools list, District wide Golden Bell winner
- **Kindergarten through Adult Education programs**
- **Integrated Service Learning**
- **Distance Learning**

The Etna Deli supports Valley Schools

TAKE AN AD

Praise, Thanks

Take out an advertisement in a local newspaper, and thank every employee by name or as a group for their contributions in building a better tomorrow (Nelson, 1994).

Date Used: ______________________ Recipient: ______________________

TEAM LUNCH

Opportunity, Respect

Allow a team of teachers to go out to lunch as a reward. You can usually get a restaurant to donate the meal if you tell them what your teachers have been doing. A lunch away from school taken at a leisurely pace will be most appreciated by your teachers. Of course with a group of teachers gone, you will have to cover their classes. You could try a large group activity outside.

Date Used: _____Recipient: _____

TELL THE BOSS

Praise, Respect, Thanks

This one is a top 20 idea. Simple, but effective.

Recognize the accomplishments of a staff member in a letter to the superintendent or the board of trustees. Send a copy of the letter to the staff member. Privately encourage the superintendent or board members to send a note back to the staff member. Getting a note from the superintendent or from a board member can be very rewarding. *I'm still waiting for my letter.*

Date Used: _____Recipient: _____

TELL THE STORY IN PICTURES

Praise, Respect

Make a photo collage showing students and staff working on a new curriculum project. Show the stages of development and its completion. Give credit to the teachers. Display the collage where it can be viewed by the public or send it to the district office for display (Nelson, 1994).

Needed: *Camera*

Date Used: _____ Recipient: _____

WHILE THEY PLAY

Thanks, Respect

This idea works best in smaller schools, but could work anywhere with some creative thinking. Gather the students into the gym or outside to participate in some pre-organized activity such as relay races, volleyball, or a schoolwide movie. While the students are being supervised by you or another administrator, invite the teachers to enjoy a good meal or pizza and time to socialize with their peers.

Date Used: _____ Recipient: _____

WHINE AND CHEESE PARTY

Thanks

Do you have a stressed-out staff going through major changes?

Bring everyone together and let them whine with some cheese and drinks. Whining is okay as long as their conversation turns to solutions before the groups leave (Connors, 2000). Sparkling cider or cranberry juice paired with a nice cheddar or Swiss can make a nice offering for a stressed out staff.

Needed: *snack food*

Date Used: _____ Recipient: _____

WINGSPREAD AWARD

Praise, Respect

Awards that are given to peers by peers are held in high regard. Here are a few examples of such awards that you can start off and then the staff members will take over and continue.

- A beautiful trophy with a winged figure is given to a "special performer." Later the person passes the award to another staff member, who is believed to deserve recognition. The recipient can keep it as long as he or she wants, or until he or she discovers another "special performer." The award can be passed on at a staff meeting or at a more formal ceremony.
- One group did the same thing with a huge, gaudy old bowling trophy purchased from a pawn shop (Nelson, 1994).
- My version of this award involved gluing three small "Cheer" laundry detergent boxes to a spray painted plate. The plate is painted gold, encrusted with jewels, and adorned with other "riches." This trophy is given from peer to peer with the required "Three Cheers" cheer. It's corny, but appreciated.

This award, no matter the form, can be very valued as it comes from the staff members. If the people doing the selection of the next recipient are perceived as having "been in the trenches," the award becomes more valued and authentic. You'll have to start the ball rolling by presenting it first. Sometimes a reminder is needed before your staff meeting so they can think of someone to honor. Rotating the award once a month seems to work well.

Needed: *A trophy of some sort. Don't be afraid of being a bit crazy.*

Date Used: _____ Recipient: _____

YOU ARE

Praise, Thanks, Respect

You can personalize your notes of appreciation or thank-yous with "YOU ARE" notes. It makes a big impact when you take the time to personalize the notes with the staff member's picture. Take a picture of every staff member interacting with students and hold on to these pictures to use throughout the year. See example in Figure 5.9.

Needed: *card stock, a picture of every staff member working or interacting with students, color printer*

Date Used: _____ Recipient: _____

FIGURE 5.9
You Are

Front of card:

Do you know what the best part of my job is?

Inside of card:

You Are!!

- 6 -

More Effort Needed, But Worth It

More Effort Needed, But Worth It

Item	Page	Thanks	Praise	Respect	Opportunity
Art Show/Talent Show	109		X	X	
Bib, Please	109	X		X	
Bonus Bucks	110	X	X		
Business Chest	110	X	X		
Family Orientation	111			X	X
Family Tree	112	X	X	X	
Fore!! Strike!!	113	X			
Gold Cards	113	X	X	X	
Heart Attack	114	X			
Honor Dinner	114	X	X	X	
Kids Say the Nicest Things	116	X	X	X	
Longfellow Lives	117	X	X		
Make Friends with the Media	117		X	X	
One-on-One	118			X	
Pamper Room	119	X			
Pay Them/Shake Them	119	X			
Paying Thanks	120	X	X	X	
Picture This	121	X	X		
Put Pen to Paper	122	X	X		
Say It with Posters	124	X	X	X	
Sing Their Praises	125		X		
Tailgate Party	125	X	X		
Take the Grading	126	X			
Teacher Grammy Awards	126	X	X	X	

Item	Page	Thanks	Praise	Respect	Opportunity
Thanks a Million	127	x			
Tongue Depressors	128	x	x	x	
Wellness Fair	130			x	
Working at the Car Wash	131	x	x		
Wrap It Up	131			x	

ART SHOW/TALENT SHOW

Praise, Respect

We are good about displaying students' art work, but why not recognize the talents of our own staff members? We all have staff members with talents that we don't see on a daily basis. Arrange for an art show of staff member works. Invite the media, display the art professionally, have soft music and sparkling apple juice.

This idea can also be expanded to include a talent show. You can ask the teachers to perform just for the students (you'll get more acts that way), or you can expand it and invite the public. The format will depend on your staff and their willingness to share their talents with the world.

Needed: *display boards, music, drinks, waiters*

NOTE: Send formal invitations to all of the district staff, families, and to the county school personnel.

Date Used: _____Recipient: _____

BIB, PLEASE

Thanks, Respect

Have a barbeque after school instead of a staff meeting. Have your secretary invite the staff's family members to come for an early dinner. It's nice to break the routine on occasion. Your PTA/PTO might pick up the tab for the food. It won't hurt to ask.

Needed: *BBQ grill, food and drinks, fuel, matches, plates, forks and cups*

Date Used: _____Recipient: _____

BONUS BUCKS

Praise, Thanks

Design a "dollar" that you can hand out to staff members who have made an exemplary effort or have done something extra for children. Once a month hold an auction using items donated by business or staff members. Be sure to include items that can be used in their staff positions or classrooms. Fun and gag items are a must. It is imperative too that bucks are given freely, but meaningfully, and that everyone has the opportunity to earn bonus bucks (Connors, 2000).

Needed: *custom made "dollars," lots of items to sell*

Date Used: _____ Recipient: _____

BUSINESS CHEST

Praise, Thanks

If you are looking for a great way to start off a meeting, look no further. Call the recognized employee up front, tell the group what they did for this honor, then let the honoree pick an item from the treasure chest.

Many local businesses will donate items that can be used as "prizes" for staff recognition. Put these in a box or chest and let the employee draw for a reward. The items could be things such as:

- Free car washes
- Pizzas
- Video rentals
- Movie passes
- Massages
- Health club passes or membership
- Meals from a restaurant

- Dry cleaning
- A round of golf
- Ski passes
- Shoe shine
- Water slide passes
- Book of the Month membership
- Beauty or barber shop coupons
- Magazine subscription

(Nelson, 1994)

Another way to use these rewards is to use the donated items for door prizes at your staff meetings. Draw a name from those staff members there on time and let that person take something from the chest.

Needed: *donations from local businesses*

NOTE: You should try for a wide variety of items. The more items you can get donated, the better.

Date Used: _____Recipient: _____

FAMILY ORIENTATION

Opportunity, Respect

This is directed towards district leadership, but it could work for principals or even department heads.

Host a family orientation event for new employees with a video program about the school district and the community. The program should not only highlight the specifics of the district but also of the community and opportunities within it. Include organizations such as Kiwanis and scouts, along with the theater guild, shopping venues, and medical facilities. Don't forget to serve refreshments. The superintendent and human resources director should attend this event.

Needed: *video describing your community and local events, snacks*

NOTE: You might have your high school drama or media class produce the video.

Date Used: _____ Recipient: _____

FAMILY TREE

Praise, Respect, Thanks

Make a large paper tree, as high and as large as possible. Attach the tree to the wall in a central area with a heading "Our Family Tree" or "You are the Apple of Our Eye." Find a quote that matches each staff member who works at your site. Attach that quote and a picture of the staff member to a paper leaf or paper apple and arrange the leaves or apples on the tree. When parents and others view the tree they will get to know your child's teacher and other school employees better. You can keep the tree "alive" by changing out the quotes with different items such as their favorite books or what college they attended. Include everyone, not just the teachers.

Needed:

- *Picture of every staff member*
- *A book of quotations*
- *Construction paper in various colors*
- *Some type of device to attach the tree to a wall*

NOTE: If you aren't crafty, you might ask a parent or the PTO members to help you.

Date Used: _____ Recipient: _____

FORE!! STRIKE!!

Thanks

- FORE!! A round of golf can be a great reward for some staff members. It also can be a fun team builder. As a team builder activity you can go on a minimum day, dividing the staff into foursomes. Have silly prizes at the end of 9 holes. Playing 18 holes is too much for beginners and will take too long. I suggest a scramble format.
- STRIKE!! A twist on the same idea is to go bowling. Bowling takes less time, money, and talent. Tell the staff to bring socks to school on the day of the outing. By only giving them that clue, it will heighten the anticipation of an adventure.

Needed: *transportation, reservations*

Date Used: _____Recipient: _____

GOLD CARDS

Praise, Respect, Thanks

Developing connections with the business owners in your town is an important aspect of any successful recognition program. Partner with local businesses to develop avenues in which the businesses give school employees a discount when they show their "School Gold Cards." Being a member of the Chamber of Commerce, Rotary, or Kiwanis is a good step towards making this idea a reality (Connors, 2000). These cards can be given out as rewards or given to all school employees as a token of respect.

Needed: *laminated cards, business connections*

Date Used: _____Recipient: _____

HEART ATTACK

Thanks

Enlist the help of your students to make hundreds of paper hearts. Cover the staff lounge walls with the hearts. Write appreciation messages and inspirational quotes on them. (I suggest writing on the hearts before you put them up.) Not every heart has to have a message, but a significant percentage should convey your appreciation. (Cathy Sork, Fort Vancouver High School, Washington, www.wacaonline.org/resources_staff.html)

Needed: *pink, red, and white construction paper; tape, book of quotes or sayings*

Date Used: _____ Recipient: _____

HONOR DINNER

Praise, Thanks, Respect

This is a way to honor teachers of older students, probably 4th grade and older.

Every teacher is chosen by at least one child or it could be by a team of two or three students. The student or team of students pays oral tribute to the teacher of their choice at an honor dinner with the teachers and their families as the honored guests. (In a high school you could have the Regional Occupational Program students or the culinary students cook the dinner.) Make sure you get a print copy of the students' tributes to present to the teachers. The dinner can be held annually or every other year. It is a great way to have the teachers hear firsthand what a difference they make in the lives of their students.

Here's another idea with the same theme:

Senior members of the Comstock High School National Honor Society (NHS) wanted to show appreciation to staff members who made a difference in their lives. From this desire to say thank you, their Teacher Recognition Dinner was born. Each senior member of NHS is allowed to invite one teacher from his/her entire K–12 experience with whom they would like to share this special evening. The program is held in the evening on the last day of school and those teachers being honored are sent invitations to attend. The name of the student inviting them is not divulged until that evening. Junior members of the NHS planned the dinner for the event. The juniors dressed up like waiters and served the seniors and their guests at the tables. The program consisted of each senior presenting a speech describing the special qualities of the teacher they selected. The teacher was then given a plaque and a copy of the speech. Many tears were shed as these students and teachers shared wonderful memories. http://michiganprincipals.org/masc/staff_appreciation.htm

Needed:

- *A student willing to speak on the behalf of each teacher*
- *A suitable venue*
- *Tables, chairs, settings*
- *Food*
- *Servers*
- *Podium*

NOTE: Send formal invitations to the honored teachers and staff members.

Date Used: _____ Recipient: _____

KIDS SAY THE NICEST THINGS

Praise, Thanks, Respect

- **Elementary:** Have all the students in a class write something nice about their teacher and include a hand drawn picture. Combine all of the notes into a book.
- **Middle and High School:** Have all the students in a home-room or first-period class write something nice about their homeroom teacher. Have them write a second letter about any other teacher in the school. Combine them into one book for each teacher. Hold a dinner for the teachers, inviting their families. Read aloud a few notes from each teacher's book and then present the books to the teachers to keep. Some of the entries will be funny and some will bring you to tears.

Needed:
- *A suitable venue*
- *Tables, chairs, settings*
- *Food*
- *Servers*
- *Podium*

NOTE: Remember to invite the family of the teachers

Date Used: _____Recipient: _____

LONGFELLOW LIVES

Praise, Thanks

This might not be for everyone. But for those who are good with a pen, this might just be the ticket.

Write a poem about an employee and his or her accomplishments. The poem could be shared privately or publicly in a newsletter or at a staff meeting (Podmoroff, 2005). If you have a poet's heart, this idea will work well for you.

Date Used: _____Recipient: _____

MAKE FRIENDS WITH THE MEDIA

Praise, Respect

Develop a positive relationship with the local media personnel in order to highlight the activities going on in your schools. "We must be our own public relations advocates in this business. The media rarely comes to us for good information, so we must go to them. The activities and staff at your schools deserve to be highlighted and the media will only do that if you have a relationship with them as they usually only are available to press the negative stuff. Take a publisher to lunch" (Connors, 2000, p. 125).

If you take pictures of the event and write the article yourself, you'll increase your chances of getting your school activities published. Plus it's more likely to be accurate and have the slant you intended.

Date Used: _____Recipient: _____

ONE-ON-ONE

Respect

This is might be a difficult one to pull off, but if you can do it, it will pay big dividends.

Listening to your employees is a great way to make them feel important and part of the team trying to meet district goals. Schedule a one-on-one meeting with every teacher in your school or district. Usually 20 minutes per person works just fine. Some meetings will take more time, some less. Have a few specific questions to ask each teacher, such as, "How is your year going?" "What do you think we need to improve?" or "How can I support you better?" but allow them to talk about anything they bring up. You will get a lot of useful information, and by taking the time you will show them that you don't take them for granted. Additionally, you will get some useful information regarding your leadership and the progress of the schools.

Sitting down for a conversation with every one of your teachers can take a fair amount of time, but the effort is so worth it. I learned an amazing amount about my new district and things that needed to be addressed. I got feedback like, "We need time to talk to each other and other grade-level teachers." This led to the institution of weekly collaboration days. Almost every teacher mentioned the need for more communication. My monthly newsletters were expanded thanks to that feedback.

> *"I felt that you valued my opinion and I was happy to talk with you."* Marie, 5th grade teacher

> *"I appreciated the time to be 'heard' and not to be criticized—hopefully the feedback helped to guide decisions."*
>
> Anonymous

Date Used: _____ Recipient: _____

PAMPER ROOM

Thanks

Set aside a space and bring in a nail technician to do the staff member's nails or to give hand massages with hot lotions. You can do this on a budget if you have a parent that works in the industry, as they will usually volunteer for the assignment. Put out a punch bowl and cookies. Play soft music. Cover each teacher's class for 30 minutes so that they can visit the Pamper Room. This isn't only for the women on your staff—the men will enjoy it too! (http://michigan principals.org/masc/staff_appreciation.htm)

Needed: *nail technician, music, punch, and finger snacks*

Date Used: _____Recipient: _____

PAY THEM / SHAKE THEM

Thanks

Deliver the staffs' paychecks in person. Shake the teacher or aide's hand and thank him or her in front of the class. The kids will most always join in and applaud the staff members' efforts. You might say, "Thank you for your efforts on behalf of our students. Here's a small token of our appreciation. I wish it were more." This process turns an impersonal act into an active recognition activity.

The classroom is quiet as I enter. The teacher is walking about the room monitoring students. I approach the teacher and ask if I may speak to the class. "Ladies and gentlemen—I am here to thank your teacher for all that she does for our school and for you. Please join with me in thanking her." As the kids clap and cheer, I hand her her paycheck. The teacher blushes and beams.

"Mrs. G is the best teacher in the school. She deserves a bonus." Called out by a fourth grade student

Needed: *time*

Date Used: _____ Recipient: _____

PAYING THANKS

Praise, Respect, Thanks

Put handwritten notes in the envelope with your employees' paychecks to recognize their contribution to the lives of children. It's best to recognize something specific, but just saying thank you works too. This can be a big task if you have a lot of employees, but it can also have a big impact. You could do it a few times a year, which would make it more manageable.

Needed: *note cards*

Date Used: _____ Recipient: _____

PICTURE THIS

Praise, Thanks

Take pictures of your staff as they work with students and post the pictures around campus. If you have access to a poster maker, it will make this project come alive. You can add captions describing the activity. See Figures 6.1 and 6.2.

Needed: *access to a poster printer*

Date Used: _____Recipient: _____

FIGURE 6.1	FIGURE 6.2
Picture This 1	**Picture This 2**

Questioning is the first step. Just ask Mrs. G.

A goal without action is only a wish. Take action. Go for it!

PUT PEN TO PAPER

Praise, Thanks

This item can empower all leaders, and I believe it is one of the most powerful ideas contained in this book.

While a genuine spoken thank-you or a verbal compliment goes a long way, it can't compare to the effect that a written note will have. Whatever the reason—a thank-you for presenting at a board meeting, a get-well wish, the acknowledgement of a job well done—the effect of your message will be increased if you put your thoughts in writing. The mere fact that you took the time to put pen to paper increases the appreciation level. When you travel throughout your school or district, you will be amazed how many of the cards you will see displayed. A written form of praise or appreciation can be reviewed and relived over and over again.

The art of writing a note is becoming extinct. The use of e-mail, social media, and cell phones has hastened the collapse of handwritten correspondence. Below are some simple and effective suggestions to make your written recognition a piece that will be read repeatedly (Saunderson, 2010).

1. **Put yourself into the note.** Write the note yourself—don't have your assistant write it for you.
2. **Handwrite the note.** A research survey conducted by the Recognition Management Institute found that receiving a note that was handwritten was the top factor for keeping a note and rereading it. Typed letters are perceived as more formal and less personal than handwritten notes. If you have to send a typed letter, add a handwritten note on the bottom.
3. **Be specific.** Let the recipient know exactly what they did to make a difference.

4. **Be prepared.** Make sure you have a supply of note cards handy—birthday cards, thank-you cards, anniversary cards, and sympathy cards. You'll need cards that have plenty of white space for adding a personal note.

5. **Act quickly.** Don't let too much time pass before you send your handwritten recognition. Being timely is an important element in making the gesture meaningful.

6. **Make it legible.** Take your time to use your best handwriting. A note that the recipient cannot read is not worth anything.

7. **Keep your intentions clear.** Be authentic and genuine and act from sincere values to show that your intentions are true.

8. **Use their names.** People feel complimented when you refer to them by name. Use their name in the body of the correspondence as well as the salutation.

9. **Express your feelings.** People say the reason they save and reread thank-you cards and letters is to recall the feelings of being acknowledged that they experienced the first time they read the card. Make sure to write your feelings for the work or actions they did.

It does take a few minutes to write a note to staff members, either as a thank-you or to recognize their contribution to the growth of children, but it doesn't take more time than it's worth. I try to write two notes a day to folks on the payroll. It doesn't have to be an elaborate note, but merely something to recognize that they are making a difference in the lives of children.

> *"Your personal notes mean a lot to me. Handwritten notes are so rare these days."*   Elizabeth, school secretary

"I appreciate receiving your notes in a time when e-mails and texts are the norm; I feel a personal written note is really special."   Maurice, 2nd grade teacher

"This really meant a lot to me. You know I go home to an empty house so your note really meant a lot."
                          Mike, continuation high school teacher

"I've saved all of the notes and cards you've sent to me. It's nice to be appreciated."   Judy, instructional aide

If you go to the dollar store you can get a box of note cards for a buck. All you have to do then is care enough to put pen to paper.

Date Used: _____Recipient: _____

SAY IT WITH POSTERS

Praise, Thanks, Respect

Make posters emphasizing the services that your support team members provide to help your students be successful. "We're better because of our instructional aides" or "Our cooks make our students healthy." Have your students come up with the text and maybe create the posters entirely. Classified employees work very hard and don't get paid a lot. This small gesture will go a long way to make them feel appreciated. If you can include pictures of your classified staff it's even better.

Needed: *poster boards, marker pens, tape, student volunteers to help*

Date Used: _____Recipient: _____

SING THEIR PRAISES

Praise

This might not be for everyone, but it can be fun.

Take the phrase "sing their praises" literally. Write a little jingle about the teacher and what she or he did. Sing the jingle at a staff meeting. It should get a lot of laughs. Present the written copy to the honored staff member. Remember, laughing is a great way to bond people.

Needed: *a good singing voice*

Date Used: _____Recipient: _____

TAILGATE PARTY

Praise, Thanks

When there is a big happening at school in the evening, whether a ball game or a play, get out the BBQ and have a tailgate party for your staff who attend the event. The booster club might be able to help you with food costs. You could BBQ some protein and have the others bring side dishes. The idea is to break bread together and to have some fun. Keep it casual. Doing this also might increase staff attendance at your extracurricular events.

The smell of hamburgers cooking on a barbeque fills the air and adds to the sounds of laughter and easy conversation. Several of the teachers and a few support staff gather in the parking lot for a pregame meal and merriment.

"You were right. I wouldn't have stayed for the game without the offer of a free dinner. I'm glad I did. It was fun. Thanks!"   Jack, 8th grade science teacher

"What a difference the game was with a group of rowdy teachers and staff in the bleachers. Everyone got into the game and the kids sure responded. Can you come again?"

John, basketball coach

Needed: *BBQ, fuel, matches, food and drink*

Date Used: _____Recipient: _____

TAKE THE GRADING

Thanks

Here's another one of my favorites.

Take home a teacher's grading for a night or a week. This will not only be a treat for the teacher, but will also give you a glimpse into how well the class and teacher are doing and if the teacher is giving immediate and timely feedback. If you find areas the teacher needs to improve, don't discuss it when you return the graded materials. It would then become an evaluation rather than a kind gesture. Wait a period of time before you approach the issue with the teacher.

Needed: *the answer key*

Date Used: _____Recipient: _____

TEACHER GRAMMY AWARDS

Praise, Thanks, Respect

Each spring, Grandville High School (GHS) holds an all-school assembly to give out "Teacher Grammies." All students vote to nominate male and female teachers for categories such as Mr. /Ms. J Crew, Bulldog (for school spirit), Energetic, Hip-and-Happenin', Sports Illustrated, etc. . . . A special "Match Made in Heaven" award is also given to a husband/wife team that work at school (there are several who qualify at GHS). The actual "Grammy" award is a certificate and a gold-painted apple which can be purchased at most craft stores. Sorting through the nominations is a tedious process but worth it when the teachers are visibly happy and excited to be recognized. This big event is the culmination of their Teacher Appreciation Week in which they recognize and show appreciation for ALL teachers. http://michiganprincipals. org/masc/staff_appreciation.htm

Needed: *student volunteers, categories, gold painted apples (not real), certificates, podium and microphone*

Date Used: _____Recipient: _____

THANKS A MILLION

Thanks

Print a real looking $1,000,000 bill (you can download one from the Internet). Electronically change as many areas as possible to make it personal, and enlarge it to avoid confusion with real currency. For example, change United States of America to your school name. Replace the face on the bill with the teacher's picture and put his/her name under the photo. Print out two copies of the bills for each teacher or staff member you want to recognize. On a large poster board print out, "Thanks a Million!" Then create the initials of the school (EHS) using the printed bills. The poster should then be displayed somewhere with lots of traffic. Each staff member should also receive a $1,000,000 bill in their mailbox.

(Barb Goll-DeWhite, Ellensburg High School, www.waca online.org/resources_staff.html)

Needed: *poster board, fake million dollar bills, glue, photo of every staff member*

Date Used: _____Recipient: _____

TONGUE DEPRESSORS

Praise, Respect, Thanks

For many employees, the recognition they most want or need is to have their boss know that they exist. Here's an easy way to make sure you connect with every employee at some point during the school year. Take tongue depressors or popsicle sticks and write one employee's name on every stick. Put the sticks with all of the names in a container on your desk. Every day draw out one or two of the sticks and go and see those people that day. You don't have to have an agenda other than merely checking in and acknowledging them and their contributions. When you finish, put the sticks in your drawer and move on to another person. The sticks are a great visual reminder and this routine will ensure that you make some personal contact with all of your employees.

If you take a few minutes to connect with your employees, it will go a long way to making them feel important and part of the team. Everyday conversations are a critical part of building relationships with your staff. You'll get to know your staff on a more personal level. You need to know about births, deaths, and illnesses so you will be able to be the cheerleader or the consoler when the times arise. To do this you must have this personal information, and the only way to get that is to talk to your staff.

The cup filled with sticks sits on my desk every day, looking back at me. It reminds me to make those employee contacts. I pull two sticks out and figure out how I'm going to be able to talk with folks today, even if only for a few minutes.

I'm always glad I have made the effort after my visits. It makes me feel more connected to the district and to my employees. I get great insight from their perspectives and often some useful gossip. The sticks slowly move from the cup to the drawer. I know I'm not going to forget anyone this way.

A comment I got from a teacher sized it up well. "Your visit today made me feel valued as a professional and as a person."   Irene, 2/3 combo teacher

By making these connections you also need to allow your employees to get to know you on a more personal level. To trust you, they have to know you. To have them willing to make changes about which they aren't completely sold, they have to trust you. They won't make a leap of faith for a stranger or merely a figurehead. Don't think you can get out of your office long enough to do this? That's bad, but it happens. Here's how I utilize the same technique with a bit of a twist. I pick 2 sticks each day and I write a quick note to these employees thanking them for what they do and letting them know they are appreciated. If you do this, make sure that you include something specific about what they do or how they do it, so they don't feel like they are getting a form letter.

Writing notes is better than nothing, but I recommend the personal visits.

Needed: *tongue depressors or craft sticks, permanent marker, container*

Date Used: _____Recipient: _____

WELLNESS FAIR

Respect

This idea uses partnerships and community connections.

Plan a wellness fair for your staff members and their families. Include community resources that can do blood work, check cholesterol, monitor blood pressure, and share healthy living techniques. Not only will this be appreciated, but it could ultimately save lives. This item has respect written all over it.

Needed:
- *Space inside or out*
- *Booths or tables*
- *Lots of volunteer presenters*
- *Advertising in the paper*
- *Invitations to the staff and their families*

NOTE: I'd suggest at least 10 booths or presenters

Date Used: _____Recipient: _____

WORKING AT THE CAR WASH

Praise, Thanks

This would be a good reward for the employee of the month. Bring your hose, bucket, and rags to the staff parking lot, and wash the recognized employee's car. It pairs nicely with a favored parking space. It's better if you do it in the parking lot rather than taking the car to a car wash. It's a bigger gesture. You can expand on this by having your entire administration team wash the cars of all of the employees in the parking lot.

Needed: *water source, buckets, rags, towels, soap*

NOTE: Make sure you remind your administration staff so they can bring a change of clothes.

Date Used: _____Recipient: _____

WRAP IT UP

Respect

Do you long to be a Christmas elf?

Set up a workstation, and wrap the gifts that the staff members are going to give out. If you are personally going to provide this service, I suggest you recognize folks with a coupon that outlines your appreciation for their services. The coupon would entitle them to your "expert" gift wrapping services for up to 10 packages during the holiday season. If you want to do this for your entire staff I suggest recruiting the help of your student council to help you wrap gifts. You should be there too. Digging in and working with the kids is a great way to build rapport.

Needed: *music, wrapping paper, tape, ribbon*

Date Used: _____Recipient: _____

~ *Appendix A* ~

Alphabetical List of Ideas

Alphabetical List of Ideas

Item	Page	EFFORT NEEDED			ELEMENTS ADDRESSED			
		Low	Moderate	More	Thanks	Praise	Respect	Opportunity
A bit of the grape	20	X			X	X		
A visit from the past	69		X		X	X	X	
Aahhh	71		X		X			
An apple a day	71		X		X	X	X	
Art show/talent show	109			X		X	X	
Ask their opinion	72		X				X	X
Attendance raiser award	20	X			X	X		
Babysitting services	21	X			X			
Balloon surprises	22	X				X	X	
Be graphic	73		X		X	X	X	
Bib, please	109			X	X		X	
Bonus bucks	110			X	X	X		
Bravo cards	23	X				X	X	

Idea	Page							
Break bread: strengthen bonds	23	x					x	x
Break the routine	74		x				x	x
Brown bag it	74		x		x		x	
Brush off	24	x			x			
Bus drivers rock	75		x		x	x	x	
Business cards	24	x			x		x	
Business chest	110			x	x	x	x	
Can't talk about work	25	x					x	
Caught in the act	25	x	x			x	x	
Certificates	26	x			x	x	x	
Clean out those files	29	x	x			x	x	x
Crosswords	75		x			x	x	
Decorate the lounge	76	x	x		x	x	x	
Don't forget the subs	76		x		x		x	
Duty calls	77	x	x		x		x	
Employee of the month	30	x				x	x	
Family orientation	111			x			x	x

Item	Page	EFFORT NEEDED			ELEMENTS ADDRESSED			
		Low	Moderate	More	Thanks	Praise	Respect	Opportunity
Family smiles	30	X			X	X		
Family tree	112			X	X	X	X	
Feature them	78		X		X	X	X	
Fore! Strike!!	113			X	X	X		
Friday focus	78		X		X	X	X	
Getting pinned	84		X		X	X	X	
Give flowers	84		X		X	X		
Go fly a kite	31	X					X	
Go put your feet up	31	X			X	X	X	
Gold cards	113			X	X	X	X	
Gone fishing	32	X			X			
Good job parents, good job teachers	32	X			X	X	X	
Great news	34	X				X		
Happy birthday	34	X				X	X	
Happy holidays	85		X		X	X	X	

Idea	Page							
Heart attack	114			X	X	X		
Hide and seek	36	X			X	X	X	
Honor dinner	114	X		X	X	X	X	
Immediate feedback	87	X			X	X	X	X
Involve them, empower them	36	X			X	X	X	X
Jeans for the day	37	X			X	X	X	
Key contributors	38	X		X	X	X		
Kids say the nicest things	116			X	X	X	X	
Let it grow	38	X			X	X	X	X
Let's eat	39	X			X			
Light up their lives	39	X		X		X	X	
Longfellow lives	117				X	X	X	
Make friends with the media	117			X		X	X	
Make that call	40	X			X	X	X	
Me bag	40	X				X	X	
Meeting agendas	41	X			X	X	X	
Mentoring programs	90	X	X			X		X

Item	Page	EFFORT NEEDED			ELEMENTS ADDRESSED			
		Low	Moderate	More	Thanks	Praise	Respect	Opportunity
Midterm break	90		X		X			
Military families	91	X	X		X		X	
No food, no meeting	41	X			X		X	
No interruptions	43	X			X		X	
One-on-one	118			X			X	
Open your house	92		X		X		X	
Pamper room	119			X	X			
Pay them/shake them	119			X	X			
Paying thanks	120			X	X	X	X	
Perk up	43	X		X	X	X		
Picture this	121			X	X	X		
Pizza anyone	44	X			X			
Place mats	92		X		X	X	X	
Plan a staff field trip	44	X					X	X
Planning days	45	X					X	X

Idea	Page							
Pot luck	46	X			X			
Pride wall	94		X	X				
Put pen to paper	122	X		X	X	X		
Put their name in lights	94		X	X	X			
Recognizing expertise	95	X	X		X		X	X
Report card reward	46	X		X				
Reserved parking	48	X		X	X			
Room service	96		X		X			
Say cheese	48	X		X	X	X		
Say it with posters	124				X	X	X	
Send them away	48	X		X	X		X	X
Shadow a teacher	97		X			X		X
Sing their praises	125			X	X	X		
Spread rumors	49	X		X				
Spread the news	49	X		X	X			
Spread the word	97		X	X	X		X	
Stand up	50	X		X	X			

| | | EFFORT NEEDED | | | ELEMENTS ADDRESSED | | | |
Item	Page	Low	Moderate	More	Thanks	Praise	Respect	Opportunity
Stressed/desserts	98		X		X			
Superintendent visit	50	X			X	X	X	
Survival kit	99		X				X	
Sweet treats	51	X			X	X		
Table topper	99		X			X	X	
Tailgate party	125			X	X	X		
Take an ad	100		X		X	X		
Take the grading	126			X	X			
Teacher Grammy awards	126			X	X	X	X	
Team lunch	101		X			X		X
Tell the boss	101		X		X	X	X	
Tell the story in pictures	101		X			X	X	
Tell us what you think	54	X			X	X		
Thank the family	57	X			X	X		
Thank the parents	57	X			X	X		

Idea	Page							
Thanks a lottery	60	x			x			
Thanks a million	127	x		x		x		
There's more to schools than just teachers	61	x					x	x
Tongue depressors	128			x		x	x	
Unexpected, The	61	x			x	x		
Wall of fame	62	x					x	
Wal-Mart cheer	62	x			x			
Welcome them	63	x					x	x
Wellness fair	130	x		x			x	
While they play	102	x		x			x	
Whine and cheese party	102	x		x	x			
Wingspread award	103	x			x		x	
Working at the car wash	131	x		x	x	x		
Working in your pajamas	63	x					x	x
Wrap it up	131	x		x	x		x	
You are	104	x		x		x	x	
You're appreciated notes	64	x		x	x	x		

~ *Appendix B* ~

Praise Ideas

Praise Ideas

Item	Page	Low	Moderate	More
A bit of the grape	20	x		
A visit from the past	69		x	
An apple a day	71		x	
Art show/talent show	109			x
Attendance raiser award	20	x		
Balloon surprises	22	x		
Be graphic	73		x	
Bonus bucks	110			x
Bravo cards	23	x		
Bus drivers rock	75		x	
Business chest	110			x
Caught in the act	25	x		
Certificates	26	x		
Crosswords	75		x	
Employee of the month	30	x		
Family smiles	30	x		
Family tree	112			x
Feature them	78		x	
Friday focus	78		x	
Give flowers	84		x	
Go put your feet up	31	x		
Gold cards	113			x
Good job parents, good job teachers	32	x		
Great news	34	x		
Happy holidays	85		x	
Hide and seek	36	x		
Honor dinner	114			x

Item	Page	Low	Moderate	More
Immediate feedback	87		x	
Jeans for the day	37	x		
Key contributors	38	x		
Kids say the nicest things	116			x
Light up their lives	39	x		
Longfellow lives	117			x
Make friends with the media	117			x
Make that call	40	x		
Meeting agendas	41	x		
Paying thanks	120			x
Picture this	121			x
Place mats	92		x	
Pride wall	94		x	
Put pen to paper	122			x
Put their name in lights	94		x	
Report card reward	46	x		
Reserved parking	48	x		
Say cheese	48	x		
Say it with posters	124			x
Sing their praises	125			x
Spread rumors	49	x		
Spread the news	49	x		
Spread the word	97		x	
Stand up	50	x		
Superintendent visit	50	x		
Sweet treats	51	x		
Table topper	99		x	
Tailgate party	125			x
Take an ad	100		x	

Item	Page	Low	Moderate	More
Teacher Grammy awards	126			x
Tell the boss	101		x	
Tell the story in pictures	101		x	
Tell us what you think	54	x		
Thank the family	57	x		
Thank the parents	57	x		
Tongue depressors	128			x
Unexpected, The	61	x		
Wal-Mart cheer	62	x		
Wingspread award	103		x	
Working at the car wash	131			x
You are	104		x	
You're appreciated notes	64	x		

~ Appendix C ~
Thank-You Ideas

Thank-You Ideas

Item	Page	Low	Moderate	More
A bit of the grape	20	x		
A visit from the past	69		x	
Aahhh	71		x	
An apple a day	71		x	
Attendance raiser award	20	x		
Babysitting services	21	x		
Be graphic	73		x	
Bib, please	109			x
Bonus bucks	110			x
Brown bag it	74		x	
Brush off	24	x		
Bus drivers rock	75		x	
Business chest	110			x
Certificates	26	x		
Decorate the lounge	76		x	
Duty calls	77		x	
Family smiles	30	x		
Family tree	112			x
Feature them	78		x	
Fore! Strike!	113			x
Friday focus	78		x	
Getting pinned	84		x	
Give flowers	84		x	
Go put your feet up	31	x		
Gold cards	113			x
Gone fishing	32	x		
Good job parents, good job teachers	32	x		

Item	Page	Low	Moderate	More
Happy holidays	85		x	
Heart attack	114			x
Hide and seek	36	x		
Honor dinner	114			x
Jeans for the day	37	x		
Key contributors	38	x		
Kids say the nicest things	116			x
Let's eat	39	x		
Longfellow lives	117			x
Make that call	40	x		
Meeting agendas	41	x		
Midterm break	90		x	
Military families	91		x	
No food, no meeting	41	x		
Open your house	92		x	
Pamper room	119			x
Pay them/shake them	119			x
Paying thanks	120			x
Perk up	43	x		
Picture this	121			x
Pizza anyone	44	x		
Place mats	92		x	
Pot luck	46	x		
Put pen to paper	122			x
Put their name in lights	94		x	
Reserved parking	48	x		
Room service	96		x	
Say cheese	48	x		
Say it with posters	124			x

Item	Page	Low	Moderate	More
Spread the word	97		x	
Stand up	50	x		
Stressed/desserts	98		x	
Superintendent visit	50	x		
Sweet treats	51	x		
Tailgate party	125			x
Take an ad	100		x	
Take the grading	126			x
Teacher Grammy awards	126			x
Tell the boss	101		x	
Tell us what you think	54	x		
Thank the family	57	x		
Thank the parents	57	x		
Thanks a lottery	60	x		
Thanks a million	127			x
Tongue depressors	128			x
While they play	102		x	
Whine and cheese party	102		x	
Working at the car wash	131			x
You are	104		x	
You're appreciated notes	64	x		

Respect Ideas

Respect Ideas

Item	Page	Low	Moderate	More
A visit from the past	69		x	
An apple a day	71		x	
Art show/talent show	109			x
Ask their opinion	72		x	
Balloon surprises	22	x		
Be graphic	73		x	
Bib, please	109			x
Bravo cards	23	x		
Break bread: strengthen bonds	23	x		
Break the routine	74		x	
Bus drivers rock	75		x	
Business cards	24	x		
Can't talk about work	25	x		
Certificates	26	x		
Clean out those files	29	x		
Crosswords	75		x	
Decorate the lounge	76		x	
Don't forget the subs	76		x	
Duty calls	77		x	
Employee of the month	30	x		
Family orientation	111			x
Family tree	112			x
Feature them	78		x	
Friday focus	78		x	
Getting pinned	84		x	
Go fly a kite	31	x		
Go put your feet up	31	x		

Item	Page	Low	Moderate	More
Gold cards	113			X
Good job parents, good job teachers	32	X		
Happy birthday	34	X		
Happy holidays	85		X	
Hide and seek	36	X		
Honor dinner	114			X
Immediate feedback	87		X	
Involve them, empower them	36	X		
Jeans for the day	37	X		
Kids say the nicest things	116			X
Light up their lives	39	X		
Make friends with the media	117			X
Make that call	40	X		
Me bag	40	X		
Meeting agendas	41	X		
Military families	91		X	
No food, no meeting	41	X		
No interruptions	43	X		
One-on-one	118			X
Open your house	92		X	
Paying thanks	120			X
Place mats	92		X	
Plan a staff field trip	44	X		
Planning days	45	X		
Recognizing expertise	95		X	
Say it with posters	124			X
Send them away	48	X		
Shadow a teacher	97		X	
Spread the word	97		X	

Item	Page	Low	Moderate	More
Superintendent visit	50	x		
Survival kit	99		x	
Table topper	99		x	
Teacher Grammy awards	126			x
Team lunch	101		x	
Tell the boss	101		x	
Tell the story in pictures	101		x	
There's more to schools than just teachers	61	x		
Tongue depressors	128			x
Wall of fame	62	x		
Welcome them	63	x		
Wellness fair	130			x
While they play	102		x	
Wingspread award	103		x	
Working in your pajamas	63	x		
Wrap it up	131			x
You are	104		x	

~ Appendix E ~
Opportunity Ideas

Opportunity Ideas

Item	Page	Low	Moderate	More
Ask their opinion	72		x	
Break bread: strengthen bonds	23	x		
Break the routine	74		x	
Clean out those files	29	x		
Family orientation	111			x
Immediate feedback	87		x	
Involve them, empower them	36	x		
Let it grow	38	x		
Mentoring programs	90		x	
Plan a staff field trip	44	x		
Planning days	45	x		
Recognizing expertise	95		x	
Send them away	48	x		
Shadow a teacher	97		x	
Team lunch	101		x	
There's more to schools than just teachers	61	x		
Welcome them	63	x		
Working in your pajamas	63	x		

References

Alliance for Excellent Education. (2005). *Teacher attrition: A costly loss to the nation and to the states.* Issue Brief. Washington, DC: Author.

Blanchard, K., & Bowles, S. (1998). *Gung ho!* New York: William Morrow.

Connors, N. (2000). *If you don't feed the teachers, they eat the students!* Nashville: Incentive Publications.

Hemsath, D. (2001). *301 more ways to have fun at work.* San Francisco: Berrett-Koehler.

Herzberg, F., Mausener, B., & Snyderman, B. (1993). *The motivation to work.* New Brunswick, NJ: Transaction.

Nelson, B. (1994). *1001 ways to reward employees.* New York: Workman.

Nelson, B. (1997). *1001 ways to energize employees.* New York: Workman.

Podmoroff, D. (2005). *365 ways to motivate and reward your employees every day—with little or no money.* Ocala, FL: Atlantic.

Putzier, J. (2001). *Get weird! 101 innovative ways to make your company a great place to work.* New York: AMACOM.

Rath, T. & Clifton, D. (2004). *How full is your bucket? Positive strategies for work and life.* Washington DC: Gallup Press.

Saunderson, R. (2010, March 10). Top 10 ways for mastering the art of recognition writing. *Incentive Magazine.*

Ventrice, C. (2003). *Make their eay! Employee recognition that works.* San Francisco: Berrett-Koehler.

Whitaker, T., Whitaker, B., & Lumpa, D. (2000). *Motivating and inspiring teachers: The educational leader's guide for building staff morale.* Larchmont, NY: Eye on Education.

Wong, H. K. (1999). There is only one way to improve student achievement. Handout from ASCD Conference.

Yerkes, L. (2001). *Fun works: Creating places where people love to work.* San Francisco: Berrett-Koehler.

About the Author

Dr. Emily E. Houck is the former Superintendent of the Scott Valley Unified School District in California. She has worked as a principal and as an assistant principal. She also has 10 years of experience as a teacher, working with special education students, regular education students, and students at risk.

Dr. Houck has received several awards from the Association of California School Administrators, including Superintendent of the Year (Region 1). She has published several articles about integrating technology into the classroom. She lives and works in northern California and is an advocate for small school districts.

You can contact Dr. Houck by e-mail at eehouck43@gmail.com.